RUBIES, DIAMONDS and GARNETS, T

A Sparkling Block-of-the-Month Quilt

By Bernadette Kent

RUBIES, DIAMONDS and GARNETS, Too ...

A Sparkling Block-of-the-Month Quilt

BY BERNADETTE KENT

Editor: Edie McGinnis
Designer: Bob Deck
Photography: Aaron T. Leimkuehler
Illustration: Eric Sears
Technical Editor: Jane Miller
Photo Editor: Jo Ann Groves

Published by:
Kansas City Star Books
1729 Grand Blvd.
Kansas City, Missouri, USA 64108

First edition, first printing
ISBN: 978-1-61169-105-4

Library of Congress Control Number: 2013946638

Printed in the United States of America by
Walsworth Publishing Co., Marceline, MO

To order copies, call StarInfo at (816) 234-4473.

Acknowledgements

Thank you to the Kansas City Star Quilts team that made this book possible.

Eric Sears has brought clarity to the instructions through his wonderful graphic illustrations. Bob Deck added his special touch and made the pages look lovely. The photographic talents of Aaron Leimkuehler and Jo Ann Groves' computer and photo editing skills added beauty to every page.

No one wants mistakes showing up in their books, and Jane Miller, our technical editor, has done her level best to keep that from happening.

Lisa Kubat, thank you for finding the little stories and histories about the precious gems.

Thanks, also, to my three lovely children Ashley Nicole, Colton Elliot and Taylor Graeme - they have learned patience waiting for me to just finish one more thing ...

A special thank you to Doug Weaver, Diane McLendon and Edie McGinnis for giving me this opportunity.

And the biggest thank you of all goes to my friend, Evelyn van der Heiden. Without her help and expertise, this book would never have made it to the printer. Thank you, Evelyn!

– Bernadette Kent

Table of Contents

About the Author

Bernadette Kent began quilting when a friend of hers, Lori Daoust, dropped by with a small project designed to keep Bernadette busy while she was home with her second child. At that time, Bernadette didn't know what a quilt was!

Her three children, Ashley Nicole, Colton Elliot and Taylor Graeme, kept her busy shuffling them to gym meets, piano lessons, soccer games, and every other event they could dream up. While she waited for each child, she stitched. As she stitched, her love of quilting grew. The more she sewed, the better she became.

In 1999, she opened a small quilt shop called Traditional Pastimes in Calgary, Alberta. She has been designing quilts, bags and miniatures since 2001.

Introduction

Rubies, diamonds and garnets – they conjure up images of luxury, wealth and beauty and have been prized since biblical days. For centuries they have been used as gifts and tokens of love and respect. The breathtaking sparkle of diamonds and the deep, dramatic reds of rubies and garnets are appealing to people around the globe.

We have a very emotional response to color. Red, in all its shades, is the color of passion, be it love, lust or hate. While managing to be gender neutral, it holds great appeal to everyone because of its bold strength.

Combine the visual appeal and forceful energy of red, toss in some white and you have the perfect combination of elements for a spellbinding quilt that, much like a perfect gemstone, will be handed down through generations.

Rubies, Diamonds and Garnets, Too ... is offered in two versions. Both were designed to use a large variety of red scraps and white or cream backgrounds. The rule of thumb for selecting the reds was that it had to read as a definite "red." The backgrounds were white to creamy white with a small red print; dots, checks, ditzies, shirtings, florals and stripes were used. The large variety of fabrics was chosen to provide depth and interest to each quilt as well as to make one take a closer look and appreciate the individuality of each fabric.

In the 13-block version of the quilt, there are 12 12-inch blocks blocks and one center medallion. This quilt was used as the 2013 Block of the Month in The Kansas City Star newspaper. The common thread that ran through the feature was reflected in the names of the blocks where little stories were told that related to gemstones and the occasions they are used.

The larger quilt uses three large medallions and 24 12-inch blocks. Half of the smaller blocks and one of the medallions were used in the Block of the Month version.

Both quilts are stunning, so make one or both. Or chose your favorite blocks and make a version particularly your own. You'll love the end result!

RUBIES, DIAMONDS and GARNETS, Too ...

VERSION 1

The quilt was designed and stitched by Bernadette Kent, Calgary, Alberta,
and quilted by Laura MacDonald, also of Calgary.

FINISHED QUILT SIZE: 68" square

Fabric Requirements

7 yards white fabric made up of:
    4 ⅛ yards of a variety of white prints for blocks
    ⅔ yard for center medallion – Fabric #3 (Cupid's Arrow)
    1 ½ yards for sashing strip triangles
    ⅔ yard for posts

7 yards red fabric made up of:
    4 ⅛ yards of a variety of red prints for blocks
    1 ½ yards for sashing strip triangles
    1 ⅛ yards for sashing strips
    ¼ yard for posts

⅝ yard white print for binding
4 ¼ yards for backing

ADDITIONAL SUPPLIES

Retayne
(We recommend you pre-wash all the fabrics in the project, separating the whites from the reds. When washing the reds, treat them with a colorfast solution such as Retayne. Be sure to follow the manufacturer's instructions for best results.)

Terminology

WOF = width of fabric
HST = half-square triangle

Note

The letter and number in parenthesis (A1) denote the shape and fabric used in each block. The letter designates the piece. The number designates the fabric. For best results, lay out all the pieces you've cut according to the diagram before you sew. Always use a ¼" seam allowance for accuracy unless otherwise instructed.

BLOCK SIZE: 12 ½" unfinished

A facet is a flat face on a geometric shape. Gemstones have many facets cut into them in order to improve their appearance. They allow the light to reflect and give a "sparkly" look to the stone. Gem cutters strive for an ideal facet cutting that displays a pleasing brilliance, strong, colorful dispersion (or "fire") and brightly colored flashes of reflected light that are called "scintillations."

Like people, gemstones have natural "flaws" that the gem cutter tries to remove or disguise when cutting the facets. In true love, each person brings out the best in the other and the natural "flaws" do not diminish the beauty within.

Fabric Requirements

Fabric #1: 6" x 14" (small red print)
Fabric #2: 5" square (white on white print 1)
Fabric #3: 5" square (50/50 print*)
Fabric #4: 5" x 9" (white on white print 2)
Fabric #5: 8" square (red background with white print)
Fabric #6: 8" square (white background with red print)

*A 50/50 print has equal amounts of red and white.

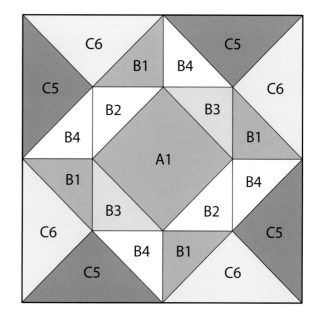

Cutting Instructions

Note: The letter and number in parenthesis (A1) denote the shape and fabric used in each block. The letter designates the piece. The number designates the fabric. For best results, lay out all the pieces you've cut according to the diagram before you sew.

Fabric #1: (A1) 1 – 4 ¾" Square
(B1) 2 – 3 ⅞" Squares - Cut in half once diagonally to make four triangles.

Fabric #2: (B2) 1 – 3 ⅞" Square - Cut in half once diagonally to make two triangles.

Fabric #3: (B3) 1 – 3 ⅞" Square - Cut in half once diagonally to make two triangles.

Fabric #4: (B4) 2 – 3 ⅞" Squares - Cut in half once diagonally to make four triangles.

Fabric #5: (C5) 1 – 7 ¼" Square - Cut in half twice diagonally to make four triangles.

Fabric #6: (C6) 1 – 7 ¼" Square - Cut in half twice diagonally to make four triangles.

Construction

For best results, lay out all the pieces you've cut according to the diagram before you sew.

1. Sew two B2 triangles to opposite sides of the A1 square. Then sew two B3 triangles to the other side of the square. At this point the block should measure 6½".

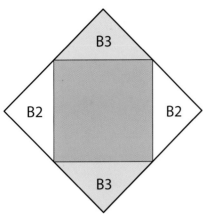

2. Sew a B1 triangle and a B4 triangle together to make the unit shown below. Make four of these B1/B4 units.

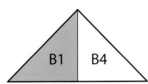

3. Sew a B1/B4 unit to opposite sides of the block. Sew the remaining B1/B4 units to the other sides of the block. At this point, the block should measure 9".

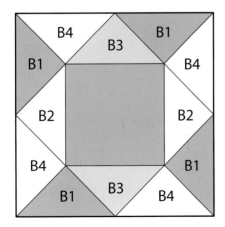

4. Sew a C5 triangle and a C6 triangle together. Make sure that the red fabric is on the left and the white fabric is on the right. Make four.

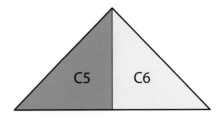

5. Sew a C5/C6 unit to opposite sides of the block. Sew the remaining two C5/C6 units to the other side of the block. The block should measure 12 ½".

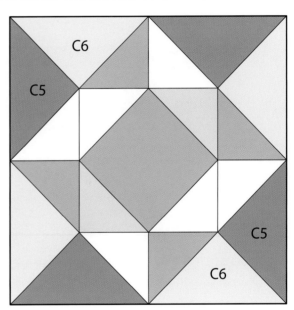

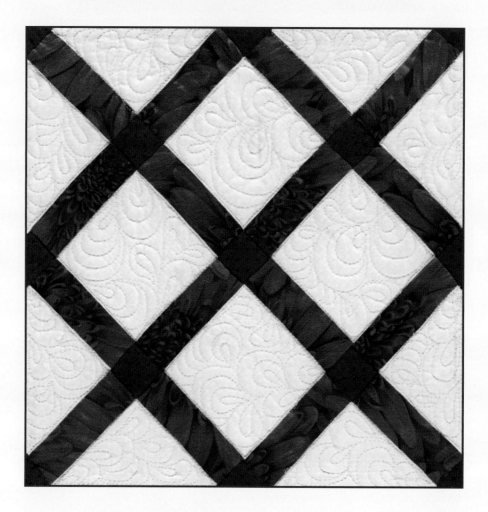

BLOCK SIZE: 12 ½" unfinished

2012 was the 100th anniversary of the current list used for birthstones. The list was defined by the National Association of Jewelers in the United States and has remained unchanged since first formulated in 1912. But the concept goes back to Biblical times to the book of Exodus.

Thousands of years ago, Moses commanded that the Breastplate of the High Priest, worn by his brother Aaron, be made using 12 colors to represent the 12 tribes of Israel. The Breastplate was a religious garment and gems matching the 12 colors were set in four rows of three: sardius, topaz and carbuncle; emerald, sapphire and diamond; ligure, agate and amethyst; and beryl, onyx and jasper.

In the first century, the writings of Flavius Josephus made the connection between the 12 signs of the zodiac and the 12 stones used on Aaron's breastplate. Each stone was said to have healing powers, and wearing the stone during its month was purported to enhance the powers attributed to it. Each month people would wear a piece of jewelry that had the gem set into it, expecting the stone to work its magic.

Wearing just the gemstone designated for a person's birth month is a relatively modern tradition that can be traced back to Poland and the 18th century when Jewish gem traders arrived in the area.

Fabric Requirements

Fabric #1: 8" x 20" (white print)
Fabric #2: 4" x 26" (large red print)
Fabric #3: 9" x 6" (small red print)

Cutting Instructions

Note: The letter and number in parenthesis (A1) denote the shape and fabric used in each block. The letter designates the piece. The number designates the fabric. For best results, lay out all the pieces you've cut according to the diagram before you sew.

Fabric #1: (A1) 4 – 3 $\frac{11}{16}$" Squares
(B1) 2 – 5 $\frac{13}{16}$" Squares - Cut in half twice diagonally to make eight triangles.
Fabric #2: (C2) 16 – 1 $\frac{9}{16}$" x 3 $\frac{11}{16}$" Rectangles
Fabric #3: (D3) 5 – 1 $\frac{9}{16}$" Squares
(E3) 1 – 2 $\frac{13}{16}$" Square - Cut in half twice diagonally to make four triangles.
(F3) 2 – 1 $\frac{3}{4}$" Squares - Cut in half once diagonally to make four triangles.

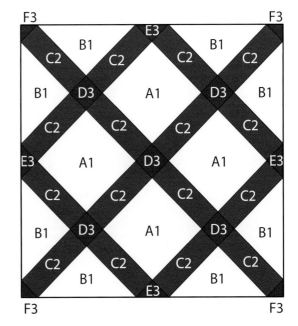

Construction

For best results, lay out all the pieces you've cut according to the diagram before you sew.

1. Sew one B1 triangle to each side of a C2 rectangle. Press towards the C2. Make two of these units.

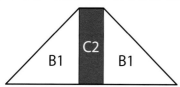

2. Sew two C2 rectangles to one D3 square.

Then add two E3 triangles to the ends of the strip. Press towards the C2 rectangles. Make two of these strips.

3. Sew two A1 squares and three C2 rectangles together.

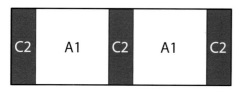

Then add two B1 triangles to the ends. Press towards the C2 rectangles. Make two of these strips.

4. Sew four C2 rectangles and three D3 squares together as shown in diagram.

5. Sew all the rows together, and then add one F3 triangle to each corner. The block should measure 12 ½".

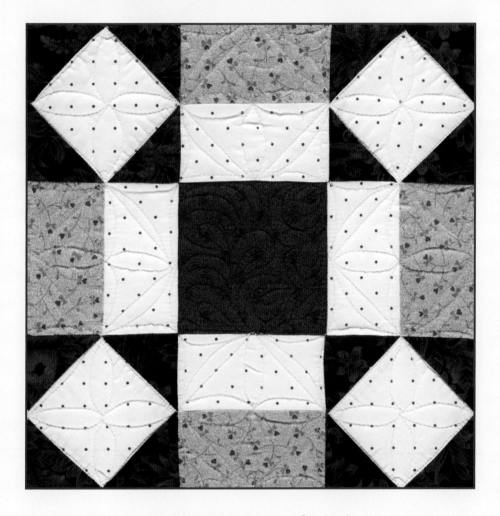

BLOCK SIZE: 12 ½" unfinished

Set as a stone by itself, a solitaire is cut to show off its brilliance and beauty. It is the most popular setting for an engagement ring and is said to signify the joining of two people becoming as one. A solitaire is the perfect setting for a large diamond. There is nothing to distract or overwhelm the beauty of the stone.

Lady Diana Spencer, Princess Grace of Monaco and Jacqueline Kennedy had solitaire engagement rings. Princess Grace was very lucky in that she had two engagement rings. Prince Rainier III of Monaco originally gave her an eternity band as an engagement ring, but upon visiting her in the United States and seeing how large and popular diamonds were, he promptly had a 12-carat emerald-cut diamond solitaire made for her.

Fabric Requirements

Fabric #1: 5" x 5" (light red)
Fabric #2: 11" x 14" (white)
Fabric #3: 11" x 5" (50/50 print*)
Fabric #4: 13" x 7" (dark red)

*A 50/50 print has equal amounts of red and white.

Cutting Instructions

Note: The letter and number in parenthesis (A1) denote the shape and fabric used in each block. The letter designates the piece. The number designates the fabric.

Fabric #1: (A1) 1 – 4 ½" Square
Fabric #2: (B2) 4 – 3 ⅜" Squares
(C2) 4 – 2 ½" x 4 ½" Rectangles
Fabric #3: (C3) 4 – 2 ½" x 4 ½" Rectangles
Fabric #4: (D4) 8 – 2 ⅞" Squares - Cut each square in half once on the diagonal for a total of 16 triangles.

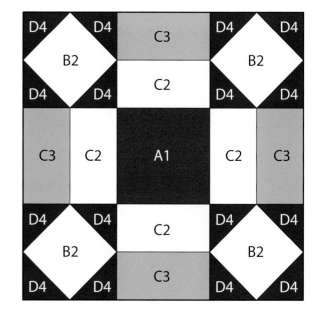

Construction

For best results, lay out all the pieces you've cut according to the diagram before you sew.

1. Pair up the C2 and C3 rectangles and sew them together. Make four of these units. Your squares should measure 4 ½".

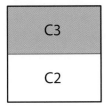

2. Sew two D4 triangles to opposite sides of the B2 square. Then sew two D4 triangles to the other sides of the square. Make four units; they should measure 4 ½".

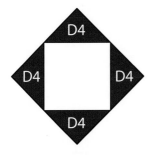

3. Lay out the units with A1 in the middle. Make sure all the white rectangles meet the red middle square. First sew three rows together vertically, then sew the rows together as shown. The block should measure 12 ½".

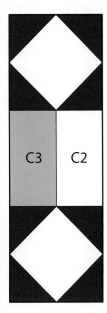

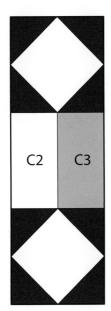

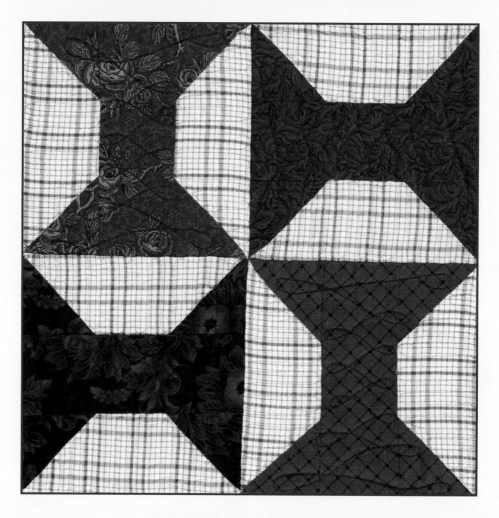

BLOCK SIZE: 12 ½" unfinished

Many little girls have dreamed of having her own pair of ruby slippers just like Dorothy in the movie *The Wizard of Oz*. There is something magical, something adventurous about those shoes! In the original book by L. Frank Baum, Dorothy's shoes were silver. The executives at MGM Studios wanted to take full advantage of the wonders of the new "Technicolor" technology and decided to make them a sparkly, ruby red.

The shoes were originally made of white silk that was dyed red. More than 2,300 red sequins and beads were attached to them. There were several pairs made for the filming of the 1936 movie but only a few are known to exist today. The ruby slippers worn by Judy Garland are one of the most asked about artifacts at the Smithsonian.

At the end of the movie, Dorothy learns that she always had what it takes to get her heart's desire, in this case the love of family, friends and the happiness of home; she just had to discover it for herself and click those ruby heels together while repeating, "There's no place like home."

Fabric Requirements

Fabric #1: 8" x 22" (light red on white plaid)
Fabric #2: 7" x 8" (red print 1)
Fabric #3: 7" x 8" (red print 2)
Fabric #4: 7" x 8" (red print 3)
Fabric #5: 7" x 8" (red print 4)

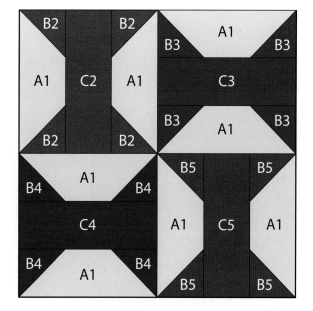

Cutting Instructions

Note: The letter and number in parenthesis (A1) denote the shape and fabric used in each block. The letter designates the piece. The number designates the fabric. For best results, lay out all the pieces you've cut according to the diagram before you sew.

Fabric #1: (A1) 8 – Pieces using Template A
Fabric #2: (B2) 2 – 2 ⅞" Squares - Cut in half once diagonally to make four triangles.
(C2) 1 – 6 ½" x 2 ½" Rectangle
Fabric #3: (B3) 2 – 2 ⅞" Squares - Cut in half once diagonally to make four triangles.
(C3) 1 – 6 ½" x 2 ½" Rectangle
Fabric #4: (B4) 2 – 2 ⅞" Squares - Cut in half once diagonally to make four triangles.
(C4) 1 – 6 ½" x 2 ½" Rectangle
Fabric #5: (B5) 2 – 2 ⅞" squares - Cut in half once diagonally to make four triangles.
(C5) 1 – 6 ½" x 2 ½" Rectangle

Construction

For best results, lay out all the pieces you've cut according to the diagram before you sew.

1. Sew two B2 triangles to opposite sides of piece A1. Make two of these units.

2. Sew the two units from step 1 to opposite sides of the C2 rectangle.

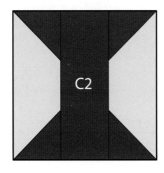

3. Repeat Steps 1 and 2 using the same fabrics for each unit (or make it as scrappy as you choose) until you have four units.

4. Arrange the four units as shown and sew them together. The block should measure 12 ½".

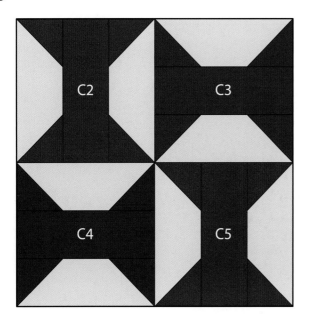

Template

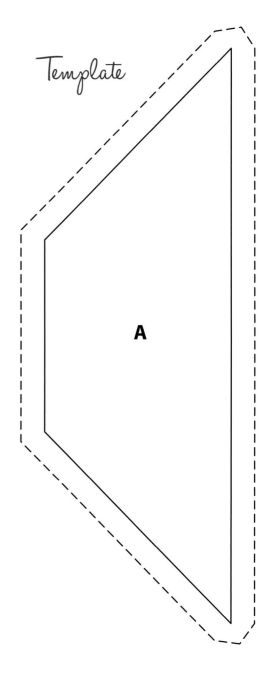

BLOCK SIZE: 12 ½" unfinished

Engagements, anniversaries, birthdays and weddings are all special occasions that call for celebrations. There's nothing like having our dear friends and family come together to rejoice in the excitement. Happiness seems to be contagious as everyone raises a toast to congratulate the celebrant.

Romantic celebrations are a golden opportunity to give a meaningful gift to a loved one. Often a piece of jewelry set with a ruby, diamond or garnet is given to commemorate a very special birthday or anniversary.

Fabric Requirements

Fabric #1: 7" x 7" (large red print)
Fabric #2: 8" x 8" (white print)
Fabric #3: 6" x 18" (dark red print)
Fabric #4: 6" x 18" (light red print)

Cutting Instructions

Note: The letter and number in parenthesis (A1) denote the shape and fabric used in each block. The letter designates the piece. The number designates the fabric. For best results, lay out all the pieces you've cut according to the diagram before you sew.

Fabric #1: (A1) 1 – 6 ½" Square
Fabric #2: (B2) 1 – 7 ¼" Square - Cut in half twice diagonally to make four triangles.
Fabric #3: (C3) 8 – Template C
Fabric #4: (C4) 8 – Template C

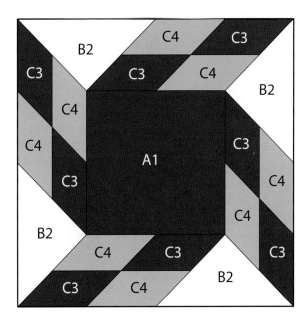

Construction

1. Pair up all the C3 and C4 pieces you have cut using the templates and sew them together to make eight pairs of each layout below. Then sew the pairs together to make four diamond units.

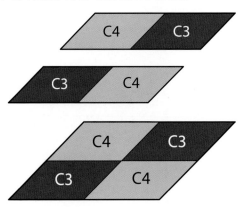

2. On the wrong side of a B2 triangle, mark the ¼" on the top point. Then mark the ¼" point on one C3 diamond and on one C4 diamond. Now sew the triangle to the diamond unit, starting the seam at the ¼" mark. Press towards the diamond unit. Make four of these side units.

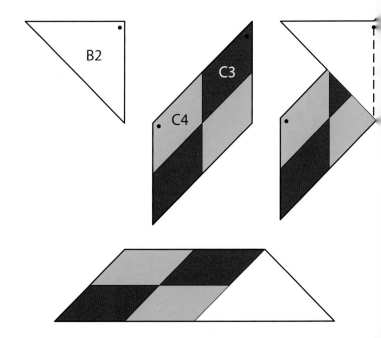

3. On the wrong side of the A1 square, mark the ¼" point on each corner. Take one side unit from step 2 and match the corner points. Then sew a seam starting and stopping at the ¼" marks. Add a second side unit to the opposite side of the square. Press the seams towards the side units.

4. Add the other two side units by matching the ¼" points. Sew the side units to the square first, then sew the diagonal corner seams, starting at the ¼" mark. The block should measure 12 ½".

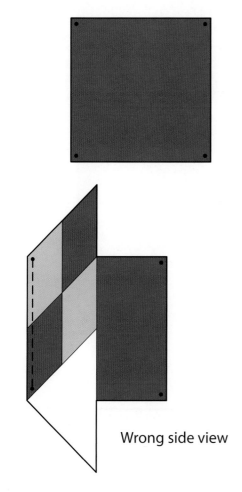

Wrong side view

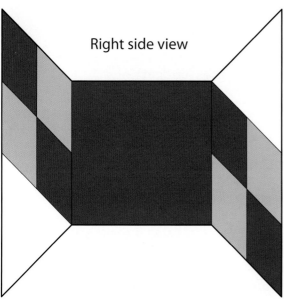

Right side view

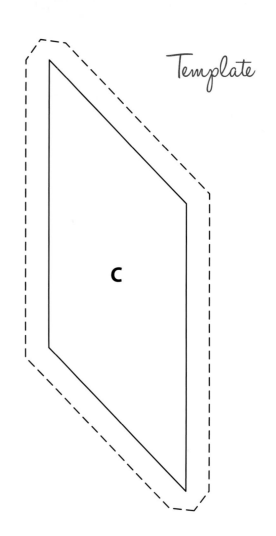

Template

C

BLOCK SIZE: 12 ½" unfinished

The happy couple exchanges rings, recites vows and with a simple, "I do," are joined together for the rest of their lives. The wedding rings exchanged between the two symbolize love, devotion and historically, an agreement between families.

The continuity of the ring represents a lasting union, and even the materials used to make it are symbolic. Diamonds are the hardest and strongest mineral on earth and can resist fire, making it the perfect material to symbolize the bond of marriage. It is worn on the third finger of the left hand because, long ago, the Egyptians believed that the vein in this finger moves straight to the heart. They thought that if their beloved wore their token, he or she was forever connected at the heart.

Wedding rings have been worn in many cultures over the centuries. While there may be variations in the traditions, the promise to love and take care of each other forever remains universal.

Fabric Requirements

Fabric #1: 9" x 18" (white on white print)
Fabric #2: 8" square (red print 1)
Fabric #3: 8" square (red print 2)
Fabric #4: 8" square (red print 3)

Cutting Instructions

Note: The letter and number in parenthesis (A1) denote the shape and fabric used in each block. The letter designates the piece. The number designates the fabric. For best results, lay out all the pieces you've cut according to the diagram before you sew.

Fabric #1: (A1) 2 – 7¼" Squares - Cut in half twice diagonally to make four triangles. You will have two triangles left over.
(B1) 2 – 3 ⅞" Square - Cut in half once diagonally to make four triangles.
Fabric #2: (A2) 1 – 7 ¼" Square - Cut in half twice diagonally to make four triangles.
Fabric #3: (C3) 2 – Diamonds using template C
Fabric #4: (D4) 2 – Diamonds using template D

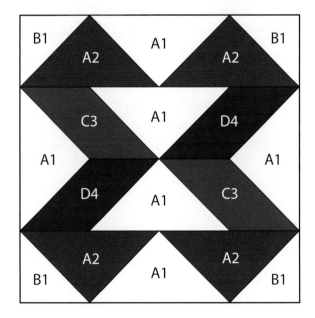

Construction

1. Draw ¼" seam lines on the wrong side of all A triangles to help ensure accurate points.

2. Sew two A2 triangles to either side of an A1 triangle. Make two of these units.

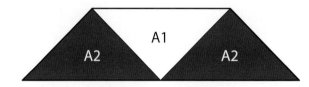

3. Sew a D4 diamond and a C3 diamond to one A1 triangle. Make two of these units.

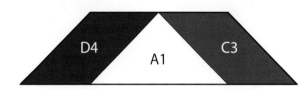

4. Mark the ¼" points on the two units from step 3. Then sew the units together as shown, starting and stopping at the ¼" points.

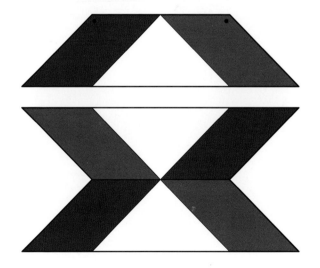

5. Attach an A1 triangle to either side of the hourglass unit with inset seams, using the ¼" seam lines and points.

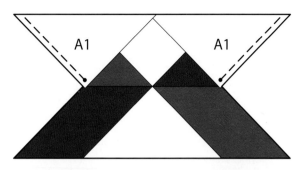

6. Sew the triangle units to the top and bottom of the center unit, and then sew one B1 triangle to each corner. The block should measure 12 ½".

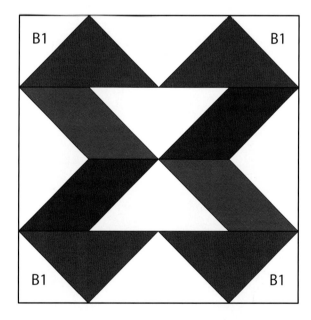

Templates

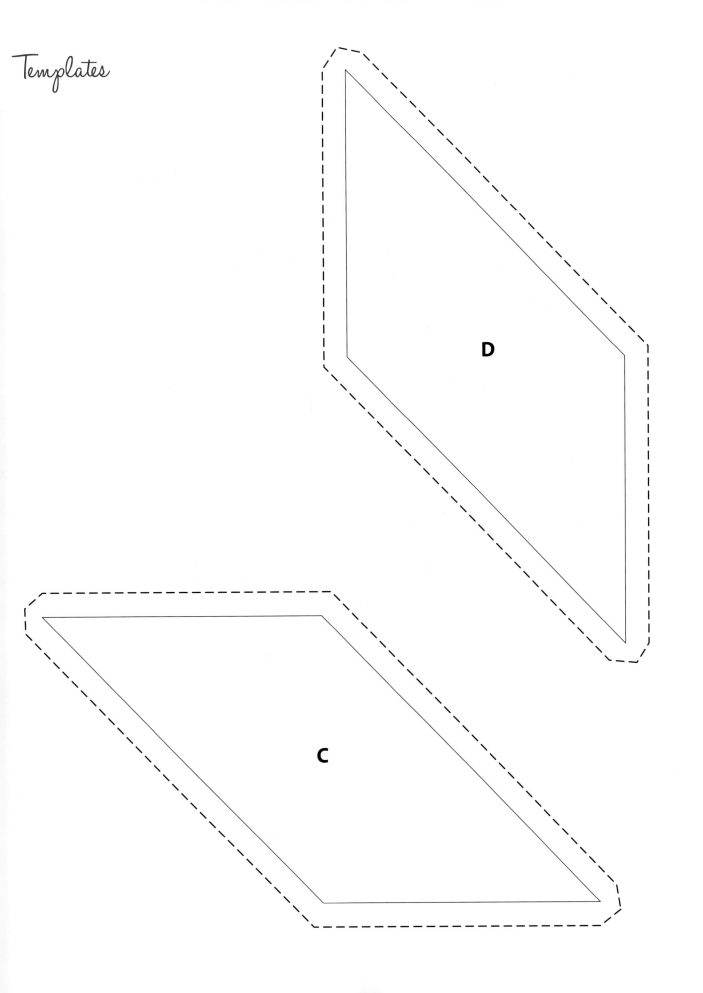

D

C

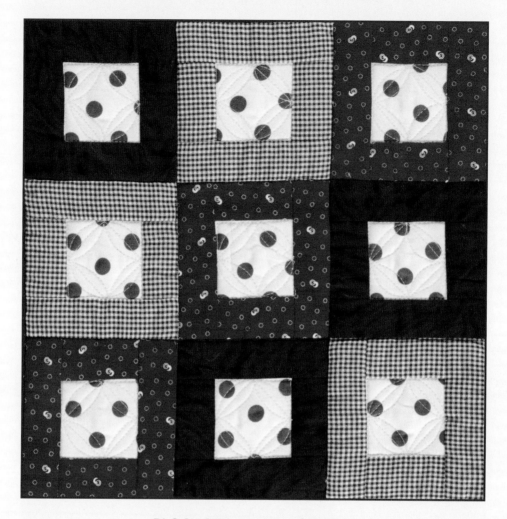

BLOCK SIZE: 12 ½" unfinished

There are many different types of cuts for gemstones, each one unique. Square cut, also known as the Princess cut, is a relatively new style created in the 20th century. Gem cutters love it because it retains 80% of the rough diamond and works well in almost style of ring.

When one compares the relationship between personality type and diamond shape, a woman who prefers a square cut diamond is usually disciplined, organized, conservative, efficient, honest and open.

Fabric Requirements

Fabric #1: 8" square (white background with red print)
Fabric #2: 6" x 15" (dark red print)
Fabric #3: 6" x 15" (medium red print)
Fabric #4: 6" x 15" (light red print)

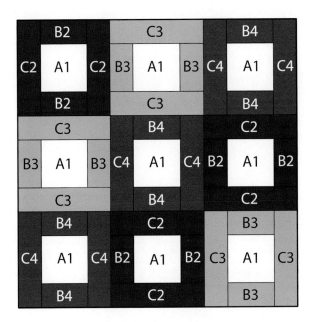

Cutting Instructions

Note: The letter and number in parenthesis (A1) denote the shape and fabric used in each block. The letter designates the piece. The number designates the fabric. For best results, lay out all the pieces you've cut according to the diagram before you sew.

Fabric #1: (A1) 9 – 2 ½" Squares
Fabric #2: (B2) 6 – 1 ½" x 2 ½" Rectangles
(C2) 6 – 1 ½" x 4 ½" Rectangles
Fabric #3: (B3) 6 – 1 ½" x 2 ½" Rectangles
(C3) 6 – 1 ½" x 4 ½" Rectangles
Fabric #4: (B4) 6 – 1 ½" x 2 ½" Rectangles
(C4) 6 – 1 ½" x 4 ½" Rectangles

Construction

For best results, refer to the photo and lay out all the pieces you've cut before you sew.

1. To make one unit, sew two B2 rectangles to opposite sides of an A1 square. Press the seams out. Then add two B3 rectangles to the remaining sides of the A1 square. The unit should measure 4 ½". Make three of these units.

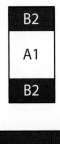

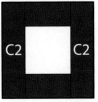

2. Repeat step 1 to make three units using fabric #3 and three units using fabric #4.

3. Arrange the 12 squares according to the diagram. Alternate the orientation of the squares (B rectangle on top, then C rectangle on the top, etc.). The block should measure 12 ½".

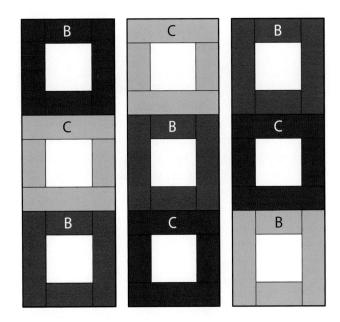

BLOCK SIZE: 12 ½" unfinished

"Hi ho! Hi ho! It's off to work we go!" Who can forget the seven loveable dwarves who opened their hearts and home to the beautiful Snow White? Thanks to the wonderful Walt Disney, they worked in a diamond mine that was a candle-lit cave with beautiful, sparkly diamonds that the dwarves chipped out with their pickaxes and hammers while whistling and singing all day.

The reality of the diamond mining business is a far cry from Disney's candy-coated version. For many years, the only sources known to man were rivers, some active and some dried up beds. In 1871, diamonds were found in South Africa and mined from kimberlite and lamproite volcanic pipes.

Some of the diamond mines in Africa were taken over by revolutionary groups who used the profits to finance the expenses for their goals, hence the term "Blood Diamonds." In 2002, the United Nations, the diamond industry and countries that bought diamonds decided to use the Kimberly process. It ensures that diamonds that are exported are documented and certified that revolutionaries have not mined the stones. Now it is very rare to have a "Blood Diamond" slip through the system and into the market place.

Fabric Requirements

Fabric #1: 5" x 9" (dark red print)
Fabric #2: 6" x 10" (white background with red print 1)
Fabric #3: 5" x 17" (red print 1)
Fabric #4: 5" x 9" (white background with red print 2)
Fabric #5: 6" x 10" (red print 2)
Fabric #6: 5" x 17" (white background with red print 3)

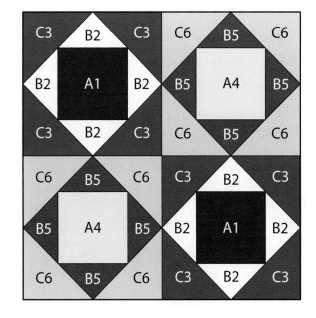

Cutting Instructions

Note: The letter and number in parenthesis (A1) denote the shape and fabric used in each block. The letter designates the piece. The number designates the fabric. For best results, lay out all the pieces you've cut according to the diagram before you sew.

Fabric #1: (A1) 2 – 3 ½" Squares
Fabric #2: (B2) 2 – 4 ¼" Squares - Cut in half twice diagonally to make eight triangles.
Fabric #3: (C3) 4 – 3 ⅞" Squares - Cut in half once diagonally to make eight triangles.
Fabric #4: (A4) 2 – 3 ½" Squares
Fabric #5: (B5) 2 – 4 ¼" Squares - Cut in half twice diagonally to make eight triangles.
Fabric #6: (C6) 4 – 3 ⅞" Squares - Cut in half once diagonally to make eight triangles.

Construction

For best results, lay out all the pieces you've cut according to the diagram before you sew.

1. Sew two B2 triangles to opposite sides of the A1 square. Press toward the center. Then sew two more B2 triangles to the remaining sides of the square. Press the seams away from the A1 square. Make two of these units.

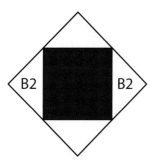

2. Sew two C3 triangles to opposite sides of the unit from Step 1. Press toward the center. Then sew two more C3 triangles to the remaining sides of the square. Press the seams away from the A1 square. Make two of these units.

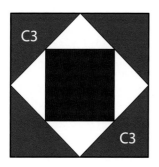

3. Repeat Steps 1 and 2 using the A4 square and the B5 and C6 triangles. Make two of these units.

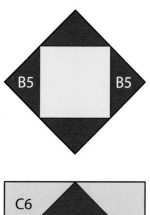

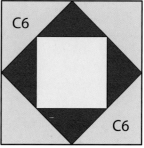

4. Arrange the four squares as shown and sew them together. The block should measure 12 ½".

BLOCK SIZE: 12 ½" unfinished

Gemstones with their lovely colors, properties and legends have been intriguing people through the ages. The pieces of mineral that have been cut and polished add spark and beauty to jewelry. Some gemstones are rarer and more expensive than others, but all have their own special attributes.

Rubies have been highly valued since biblical times. They were set into the gold coronation ring of English kings and can also be found in the crowns, scepters and royal jewels of many other nations. Rubies are viewed as a symbol of freedom, charity, dignity and divine power. Only diamonds are harder than rubies.

Diamonds are the hardest, most imperishable and brilliant of all the gemstones. The word "diamond" comes from the Greek word "adamas" meaning unconquerable. Even though this stone has been the source of fascination for centuries, it is made from carbon, one of the most common elements on Earth.

Garnets are sometimes called the "rainbow of gemstones" because they can be found in every color, although red is the most common. They are considered to be a gem of faith, constancy and truth. Garnets have traditionally been a popular and classic choice for men's accessories, such as rings, tie tacks and cufflinks as the deep red color beautifully accents traditional male suit colors.

Fabric Requirements

Fabric #1: 11" x 14" (white on white print)
Fabric #2: 9" x 14" (red print 1)
Fabric #3: 9" x 14" (red print 2)

Cutting Instructions

Note: The letter and number in parenthesis (A1) denote the shape and fabric used in each block. The letter designates the piece. The number designates the fabric. For best results, lay out all the pieces you've cut according to the diagram before you sew.

Fabric #1: (A1) 18 – Triangles using template A
Fabric #2: (B2) 9 – Pieces using template B
Fabric #3: (B3) 9 – Pieces using template B

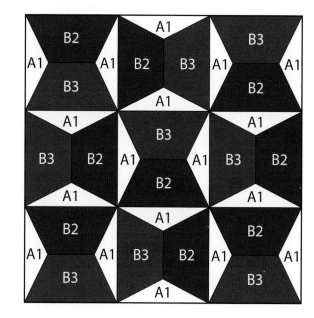

Construction

For best results, lay out all the pieces you've cut according to the diagram before you sew.

1. On the wrong side of the pieces, mark the ¼" point on all A and B pieces as shown.

2. To make one square, pair up a B2 piece and a B3 piece. Sew them together along the short sides, starting and stopping at the ¼" marks. Now add two A1 triangles, using an inset seam and beginning at the center point on each side. The unit should measure 4 ½". Make a total of nine of these units.

3. Arrange the squares into 3 rows of 3 blocks and sew them together. You can orient them as in the diagram or make up your own arrangement. The block should measure 12 ½".

Templates

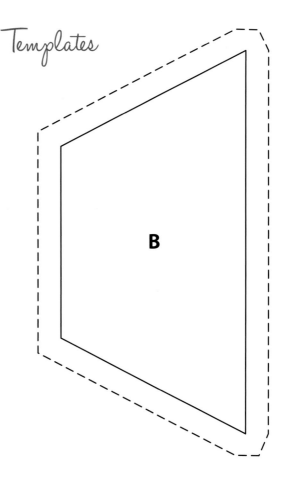

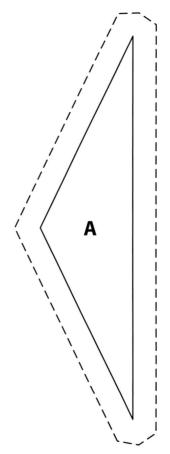

BLOCK SIZE: 12 ½" unfinished

Founded in 1837 by Charles Tiffany and Teddy Young, Tiffany & Co is renowned for luxury goods, especially its diamonds and jewelry. Known for its high standards, it is considered to be the epitome of classic elegance. Tiffany jewelry has bedecked some of the most illustrious and wealthiest families including the Astors, Vanderbilts, Posts, Huttons and Morgans. Actresses such as Kate Winslet, Angelina Jolie and Anne Hathaway have worn Tiffany creations while filming movies as well as strolling down red carpets at Hollywood premieres.

The famous Tiffany Diamond is a stunning 128-carat yellow diamond and is said to have been worn only two times. Mrs. Sheldon Whitehouse was the first woman to step out wearing the lovely jewel when she attended the Tiffany Ball in Newport, Rhode Island, in 1957. Audrey Hepburn wore it for a promotional picture for the 1961 movie, *Breakfast at Tiffany's*.

The store has been mentioned or featured in several popular songs and movies of the 20th century, such as *Diamonds are a Girl's Best Friend* sung by Marilyn Monroe in the movie *Gentlemen Prefer Blondes* and Eartha Kitt in her classic Christmas song, *Santa Baby*.

Tiffany's is a store that appeals to everyone for its reputation of quality, excellence and elegance. Even their packaging is famous – little blue boxes with a white satin bow.

Fabric Requirements

Fabric #1: 8" x 12" (red print 1)
Fabric #2: 8" x 23" (50/50 print*)
Fabric #3: 8" x 13" (white on white print)
*A 50/50 print has equal amounts of red and white.

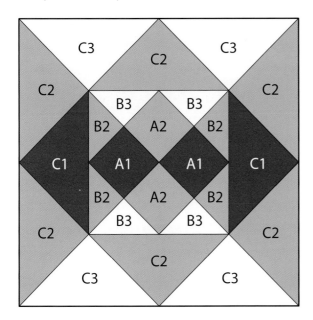

Cutting Instructions

Note: The letter and number in parenthesis (A1) denote the shape and fabric used in each block. The letter designates the piece. The number designates the fabric. For best results, lay out all the pieces you've cut according to the diagram before you sew.

Fabric #1: (A1) 2 – 2 ⅝" Squares
(C1) 1 – 7 ¼" Square - Cut in half twice diagonally to make four triangles (only need two).

Fabric #2: (A2) 2 – 2 ⅝" Squares
(B2) 1 – 4 ¼" Square - Cut in half twice diagonally to make four triangles.
(C2) 2 – 7 ¼" Square - Cut in half twice diagonally to make eight triangles (only need six).

Fabric #3: (B3) 1 – 4 ¼" Square - Cut in half twice diagonally to make four triangles.
(C3) 1 – 7 ¼" Square - Cut in half twice diagonally to make four triangles.

Construction

For best results, lay out all the pieces you've cut according to the diagram before you sew.

1. To begin, sew the two A1 and two A2 squares into a 4-patch.

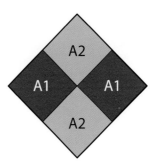

2. Pair up the B2 and B3 triangles. For two of the pairs, the white triangle is on the right side and for the other two pairs, the white triangle is on the left side.

White on the right side.

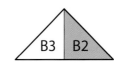

White on the left side.

3. To attach the triangle units to the 4-patch, position them so the white B3 triangles are always next to the 50/50 print A2 squares. First sew on two triangle units to opposite sides of the 4-patch, and then sew the remaining two triangle units in place as shown.

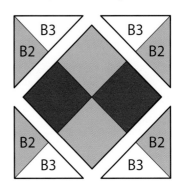

4. Next, add the C1 triangles to the B2 sides of the block. Then add the C2 (50/50 print) triangles to the B3 (white) sides.

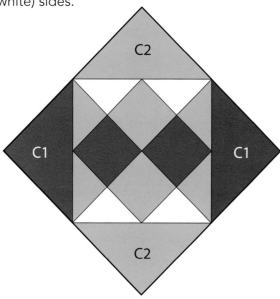

6. Repeat Step 3 to attach the corners. Be sure to watch the placement. The block should measure 12 ½".

5. To make the outer corners, pair up the C2 and C3 triangles, just as in Step 2, making two units of each.

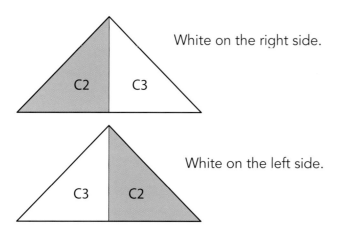

White on the right side.

White on the left side.

BLOCK SIZE: 12 ½" unfinished

Cartier is considered one of the premier jewelers in the world. The business was founded in 1847 by Louis-Francois Cartier (1819-1904) in Paris. In 1874, his son, Alfred, took over but it wasn't until his sons, Louis, Pierre and Jacques, joined the family business that the Cartier brand was established worldwide.

Perhaps the most famous jewel to pass through Pierre Cartier's hands was the Blue Hope Diamond. In 1911, it was sold to American Evalyn Walsh McLean. She was shown the diamond at the shop in Paris but wasn't fond of the setting. Cartier had the diamond reset and took it to the United States and left it with McLean for the weekend. It turned out to

be a brilliant sales strategy; she purchased the jewel that she kept until she passed away in 1947.

Cartier might have worked one of the best real estate deals ever in 1917 when their New York store moved from 712 Fifth Avenue, New York, New York, to 653 Fifth Avenue (Morton S. Plant's mansion) in exchange for $100 and a double-strand necklace of natural pearls. One strand had 55 pearls, the second, 73. The necklace was said to be valued at $1,000,000, an enormous sum at the time.

Fabric Requirements

Fabric #1: 8" x 22" (white on white print)
Fabric #2: 8" x 11" (red print 1)
Fabric #3: 10" x 11" (red print 2)

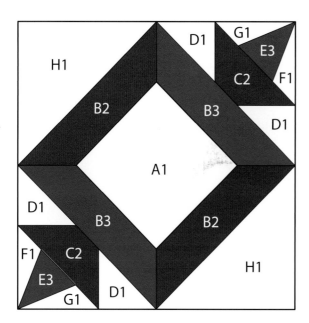

Cutting Instructions

Note: The letter and number in parenthesis (A1) denote the shape and fabric used in each block. The letter designates the piece. The number designates the fabric. For best results, lay out all the pieces you've cut according to the diagram before you sew.

Fabric #1: (A1) 1 – 5 ⁷⁄₁₆" Square
(D1) 2 – 3 ⅜" Squares - Cut in half once diagonally to make four triangles.
(F1) 2 – Triangles using template F
(G1) 2 – Triangles using template G
(H1) 1 – 6 ⅞" square - Cut in half once diagonally to make two triangles.
Fabric #2: (B2) 2 – Pieces using template B
(C2) 2 – Pieces using template C
Fabric #3: (B3) 2 – Pieces using template B
(E3) 2 – Triangles using template E

Construction

For best results, lay out all the pieces you've cut according to the diagram before you sew.

1. Mark the ¼" points on the reverse side of the B2 and B3 pieces as shown below.

2. To start the block, sew both B2 pieces to opposite sides of the A1 square – starting and stopping at the ¼" marks. Then add the B3 pieces. Sew to the ¼" mark. Miter the corners by stitching from the inside point to the outside edge. The unit should measure 9".

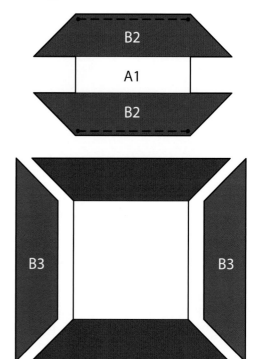

3. To make a pieced corner, sew two D1 triangles to a C2 piece. Next, sew an F1 triangle and a G1 triangle to an E3 triangle. Now sew the E3 unit to the top of the C2 unit. Make two.

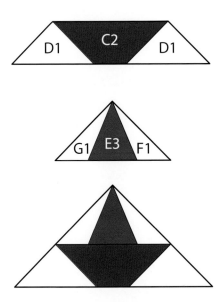

4. Sew the pieced corner units from step 3 to the B3 sides of the square. Then sew the H1 triangles to the remaining sides. The block should measure 12 ½".

Templates

E

B

F

C

G

BLOCK SIZE: 12 ½" unfinished

For nearly 100 years, the Round Brilliant Cut Diamond has been the best selling diamond on the market. The first brilliant cuts were introduced in the middle of the 17th century. The actual shape is like a cone and has facets that are shaped like triangles and kites. The facets are positioned outward allowing as much light as possible to shine through, thus creating exceptional brilliance or sparkle.

The most popular type of engagement ring is a round brilliant. According to research into the relationship between personality type and diamond shape, a woman who prefers a round brilliant cut diamond is home- and family-centered, dependable, relaxed, easy to get along with, and security conscious.

Fabric Requirements

Fabric #1: 12" x 21" (red on white print)
Fabric #2: 8" x 24" (red print 1)
Fabric #3: 7" x 7" (red print 2)

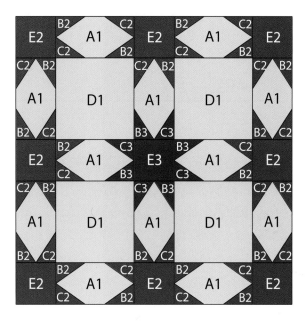

Cutting Instructions

Note: The letter and number in parenthesis (A1) denote the shape and fabric used in each block. The letter designates the piece. The number designates the fabric. For best results, lay out all the pieces you've cut according to the diagram before you sew.

Fabric #1: (A1) 12 – Pieces using template A
(D1) 4 – 3 ⅞" Squares

Fabric #2: (B2) 10 – 1 ⅝" x 2 ⅜" Rectangles - Cut in half diagonally (top right to bottom left corner) once to make 20 triangles.
(C2) 10 – 1 ⅝" x 2 ⅜" Rectangles - Cut in half diagonally (top left to bottom right corner) once to make 20 triangles.
(E2) 8 – 2 ¼" Squares

Fabric #3: (B3) 2 – 1 ⅝" x 2 ⅜" Rectangles - Cut in half diagonally (top right to bottom left corner) once to make 4 triangles.
(C3) 2 – 1 ⅝" x 2 ⅜" Rectangles - Cut in half diagonally (top left to bottom right corner) once to make 4 triangles.
(E3) 1 – 2 ¼" Square

Construction

For best results, lay out all the pieces you've cut according to the diagram before you sew.

1. Sew two B2 triangles to opposite sides of an AI template. Then sew two C2 triangles to the remaining sides of the template. Make eight of these fabric 2/2 units.

2. Sew a B2 triangle and a C2 triangle to one end of an AI template. Then sew a B3 triangle and a C3 triangle to the opposite end of the template. Make four of these fabric 2/3 units.

3. Sew two fabric 2/2 units and three E2 squares together in a row as shown in the diagram. Make two of these rows.

4. Sew two fabric 2/3 units, two E2 squares and one E3 square together in a row as shown in the diagram.

5. Sew two fabric 2/2 units, one fabric 2/3 unit and two D1 squares together in a row as shown. Make two of these rows.

6. Sew the rows together, forming a dark red star in the middle of the block. The block should measure 12 ½".

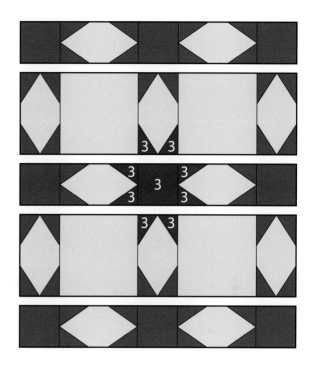

Template

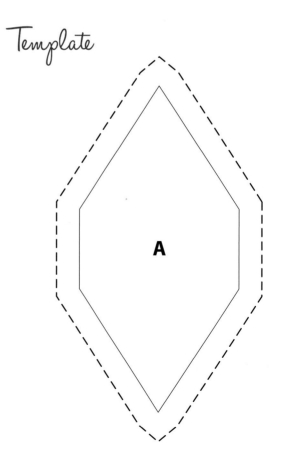

BLOCK SIZE: 28 ½" unfinished

Cupid has long been a symbol for love and is often portrayed as a mischievous, playful, winged child whose arrows carry the power to induce love. Some myths say that he shoots two hearts with one arrow, thereby joining two lives in love. But Cupid has two sets of arrows in his quiver: a set that has gold-tipped arrows that creates true love and a lead-tipped set that creates lust.

In Greek mythology, Cupid was known as Eros and was the son of Aphrodite. In Roman mythology, he was called Cupid and was the son of Venus. Cupid married his true love, Psyche (meaning "soul"). The path to marriage was not easy for Cupid and Psyche, as Venus was jealous of her beauty and wanted to destroy her. The two endured impossible trials to be together. The gods were so impressed with Psyche and Cupid's deep love that they made her a goddess so the two could be properly married, proving true love will endure.

Fabric Requirements

Fabric #1: 12" x 20" (small red print on white 1)
Fabric #2: 14" x 20" (dark red)
Fabric #3: 6" x 14" (light red)
Fabric #4: 6" x 14" (red print 1)
Fabric #5: 6" square (red print on white)
Fabric #6: 6" square (white print on red)
Fabric #7: 6" x 10" (red polka dot)
Fabric #8: 9" x 20" (red print 2)
Fabric #9: ⅝ yard (small red print on white 2)

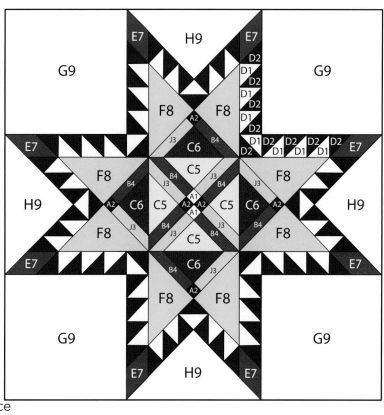

Cutting Instructions

Fabric #1: (A1) 2 – 1 ⁵⁄₁₆" Squares
(D1) 24 – 2 ½" Squares - Cut in half once diagonally to make 48 triangles.

Fabric #2: (A2) 6 – 1 ⁵⁄₁₆" Squares
(D2) 32 – 2 ½" Squares - Cut in half once diagonally to make 64 triangles.

Fabric #3: (J3) 8 – Pieces using template J

Fabric #4: (B4) 8 – Pieces using template B

Fabric #5: (C5) 1 – 5 ¹¹⁄₁₆" Square - Cut in half twice diagonally to make four triangles.

Fabric #6: (C6) 1 – 5 ¹¹⁄₁₆" Square - Cut in half twice diagonally to make four triangles.

Fabric #7: (E7) 8 – Diamonds using template E

Fabric #8: (F8) 2 – 7 ¹⁵⁄₁₆" Squares - Cut in half twice diagonally to make eight triangles.

Fabric #9: (G9) 4 – 9 ⁷⁄₁₆" Squares
(H9) 1 – 11 ⁵⁄₁₆" Square - Cut in half twice diagonally to make four triangles.

Construction

1. To make the center, begin by sewing a B4 piece to an Al square. Then sew a C5 triangle to a J3 piece. Join the two units as shown. Make two.

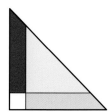

2. Now sew a B4 piece to an A2 square. Make six. Set four aside. Now sew a C5 triangle to a J3 piece. Sew the remaining A2/B4 units to a C5/J3 unit as shown. Make two of these units.

3. Sew an A1 unit from step 1 to an A2 unit from step 2 as shown. Make two. To complete the square, sew the two units together as shown.

4. Sew a C6 triangle to a J3 piece. Make four. Take the remaining A2/B4 units from step 2 and sew to the left side of the C6/J3 triangle you just made. Make four of these units.

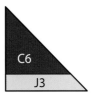

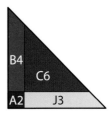

5. To complete the center square, sew a C6 unit to opposite sides of the block. Sew the remaining C6 units to the other sides of the block. At this point, the block should measure 10" unfinished.

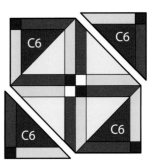

6. To make the feathered points, you need 48 half-square triangle units. Pair up a D1 triangle with a D2 triangle, and sew them together on the diagonal. Chain-piece the triangles to make a total of 48 – 2 ⅛" unfinished half-square triangle units.

7. To make a corner unit, make a strip of four half-square triangle units and one D2 triangle as shown. Now make another strip of three half-square triangle units and one D2 triangle as shown. When making the strips for this step, sew the seams with a scant ¼" seam allowance. Beginning with the smaller strip, sew them to a G9 square with a partial seam (sew only where indicated by the dark lines). Make four of these units.

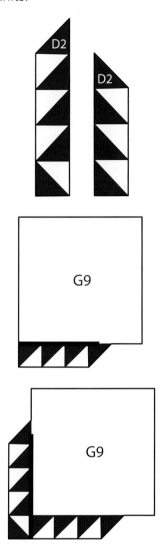

Now add two F8 triangles to either side of a G9 unit as shown. Make four of these units. Set aside.

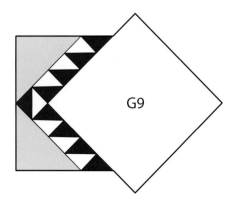

8. To make a side unit, make a strip of three half-square triangle units, a D2 triangle and an E7 diamond as shown. Now make another strip of two half-square triangle units, a D2 triangle and an E7 diamond as shown. When making the strips for this step, sew the seams with a generous ¼" seam allowance. Beginning with the smaller strip, sew them to an H9 triangle. Make four of these units.

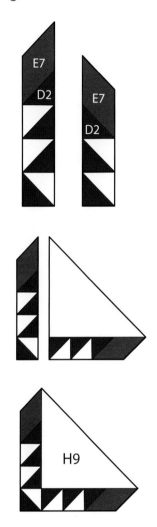

9. Join two side and one corner unit as shown. Stitch the seams in the order indicated by the dark lines to complete the partial seams. Make two of these units.

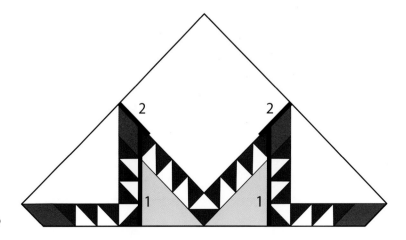

10. To complete the block, first add a corner unit from Step 7 to opposite sides of the center square as shown. Then sew a unit from step 9 to each remaining side of the center unit. Stitch the seams closed where indicated by the dark lines to complete the partial seams.

Templates

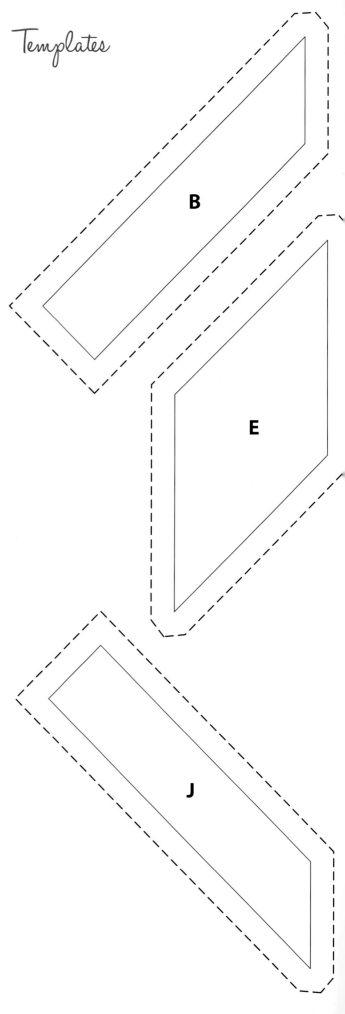

B

E

J

Finishing Instructions

Sashing Strips

BLOCK SIZE: 4 ½" x 12 ½" unfinished

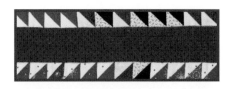

Fabric Requirements

Fabric #1: 1 ½ yards (red) - Use an assortment of prints for a scrappy look.

Fabric #2: 1 ½ yards (white) - Use an assortment of prints for a scrappy look.

Fabric #3: 1 ⅛ yards (red) - Use an assortment of prints for a scrappy look.

Cutting Instructions

Fabric #1: 22 – 1 ⅞" Strips - Cut the strips into 432 – 1 ⅞" squares. Cut in half once diagonally to make 864 triangles.

Fabric #2: 22 – 1 ⅞" Strips - Cut the strips into 432 – 1 ⅞" squares. Cut in half once diagonally to make 864 triangles.

Fabric #3: 36 – 2 ½" x 12 ½" Rectangles

Construction

Pair up a fabric #1 with a fabric #2 triangle and sew together on the diagonal. Chain-piece the triangles to make a total of 864 – 1 ½" unfinished half-square triangle units.

For the sawtooth sashing strips, you should have 864 half-square triangle units and 36 – 2 ½" x 12 ½" rectangles. Now you can start putting the sawtooth sashing strips together.

1. Randomly select 12 half-square triangle units and sew them together into a strip. Refer to the diagram below for proper placement of the red and white triangles. Make 36 of these A strips.

2. Randomly select another 12 half-square triangle units and sew them together into a strip. Refer to the diagram for proper placement of the red and white triangles. Notice that the color position of the half-square triangle units in this strip is the opposite of strip A. Make 36 of these B strips.

3. To make a sawtooth sashing strip, randomly select one A strip, one B strip and one rectangle (2 ½" x 12 ½"). First, sew the A strip to the red rectangle. Make sure the white triangles are beside the red rectangle.

Next sew the B strip to the other side of the rectangle. Again, make sure the white triangles are beside the red rectangle. Make 36 sawtooth sashing strips.

Posts

BLOCK SIZE: 4 ½" unfinished

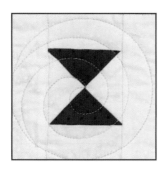

Fabric Requirements

Note: Fabrics #2, #3 and #4 can be the same white print or you can mix them up.

Fabric #1: 8" x 26" (red print)
Fabric #2: 8" x 26" (white print)
Fabric #3: 6" x WOF (white print)
Fabric #4: 10" x WOF (white print)

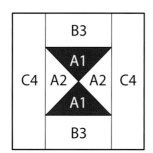

Cutting Instructions

Note: The letter and number in parenthesis (A1) denote the shape and fabric used in each block. The letter designates the piece. The number designates the fabric. For best results, lay out all the pieces you've cut according to the diagram before you sew.

Fabric #1: (A1) 12 – 3 ¼" Squares - Cut in half twice diagonally to make 48 triangles.
Fabric #2: (A2) 12 – 3 ¼" Squares - Cut in half twice diagonally to make 48 triangles.
Fabric #3: (B3) 48 – 2 ½" x 1 ½" Rectangles
Fabric #4: (C4) 48 – 4 ½" x 1 ½" Rectangles

Construction

1. To make the hourglass center, pair up all the A1 and A2 triangles. Make sure the red fabric is always on the left and the white fabric is always on the right. Sew them together and press toward the red fabric. Make two of these units, then join them to make a square. Make 24 hourglass squares.

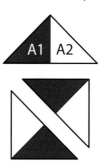

2. Sew two B3 rectangles to the red sides of an hourglass square. Then sew two C4 rectangles to the white sides of the hourglass square. This block should measure 4 ½" square. Make 24 units.

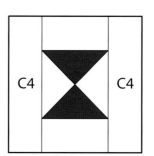

Construction

1. We recommended you lay out the entire quilt before sewing everything together. The sashing strips are directional due to the half-square triangle placement and you should orient them in the manner you find most visually appealing.

2. To begin, start by sewing the sashing rows together. Sew five posts and four sashing strips together as shown in the diagram. Make four of these units. Note: all the posts in our quilt were not oriented in the same position. Place them however you like.

3. Next create the top and bottom rows of blocks. Sew sashing strips to the sides of four blocks as shown in the diagram. Make one of each of these units.

4. Now sew a sashing strip to either side of the four blocks shown in the diagram. Put aside until later.

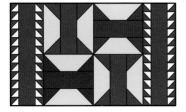  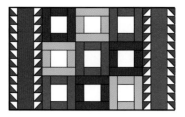 

5. Sew a sashing strip between two posts. Make two of these units.

6. Next, sew a sashing strip unit from step 5 between two of the block units from step 4 as shown in the diagram. Be sure you have the correct placement of the blocks before sewing.

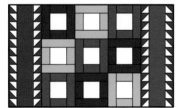 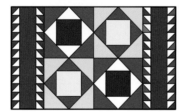

7. Use the units from Step 6 and sew them to either side of the center medallion as shown in the diagram below.

8. You now have all the pieces to put together the final quilt. Sew together in rows to create the final project as shown in the diagram below.

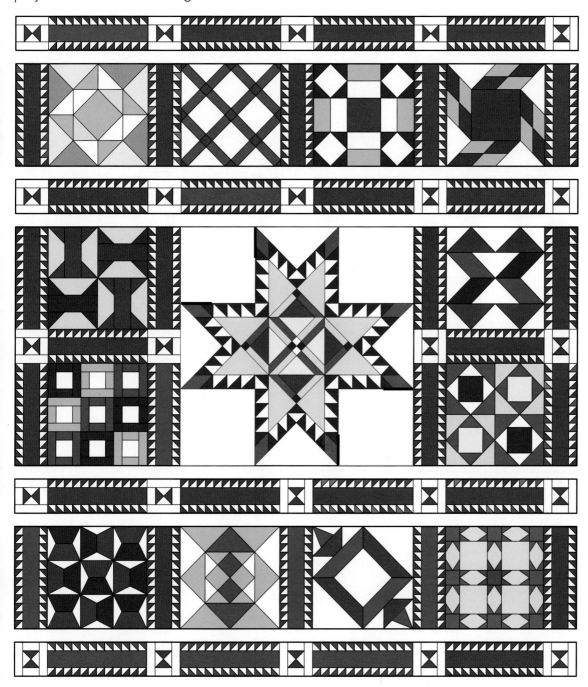

9. Layer the quilt with batting, backing and quilt. Trim and bind.

RUBIES, DIAMONDS and GARNETS, Too ...
VERSION 2

Made by Bernadette Kent, Calgary, Canada | Quilted by Lorraine Appleby, Calgary, Canada

FINISHED QUILT SIZE: 100" square

Fabric Requirements

11 yards white fabric made up of:
- 6 yards of a variety of white prints for blocks
- 2 yards of a variety for the three feature blocks
  (Cupid's Arrow, Two Months Salary, Fire and Ice)
- 2 ⅓ yards for sashing strip triangles
- ⅔ yard for posts

11 ⅓ yards red fabric made up of:
- 4 yards of a variety of red prints for blocks
- 2 yards of a variety for the three feature blocks
  (Cupid's Arrow, Two Months Salary, Fire and Ice)
- 1 ½ yards for sashing strip triangles
- 4 yards for sashing strips
- 1 ¾ yards for center sashing
- 2 ¼ yards for half-square triangles
- ¼ yard for posts

⅝ yard for binding
9 yards for backing

ADDITIONAL SUPPLIES
Retayne

A Few Notes Before You Begin

We recommend you pre-wash all the fabrics in the project, separating the whites from the reds. When washing the reds, treat them with a colorfast solution such as Retayne. Be sure to follow the manufacturer's instructions for best results.

Read all the instructions before you cut the pieces for each block.

Lay out all the pieces you've cut according to the diagram before you sew.

Always use a ¼" seam allowance for accuracy, unless instructed otherwise.

Refer to Rubies, Diamonds and Garnets, Too... Version 1 for instructions for Blocks 1–13 on pages 6–48.

BLOCK SIZE: 28 ½" unfinished

Fabric Requirements

Fabric #1: 8" x 12" (dark red 1)
Fabric #2: 8" x 12" (red print on white)
Fabric #3: 5" x 15" (small red print on white)
Fabric #4: 5 ½" x WOF (dark red 2)
Fabric #5: ¼ yard (white print 1)
Fabric #6: 10" x 42" (red print)
Fabric #7: ⅝ yard (white print 2)

Cutting Instructions

Fabric #1: (A1) 4 Triangles using template A

Fabric #2: (A2) 4 Triangles using template A

Fabric #3: (B3) 4 – 3 ⅜" Squares - Cut in half once diagonally to make eight triangles.

Fabric #4: (H4) Cut 28 - 2 ⅜" Squares - Cut the squares in half once diagonally to make 56 triangles.

Fabric #5: (H5) Cut 36 - 2 ⅜" Squares - Cut in half once diagonally to make 72 triangles.

Fabric #6: (D6) 4 Pieces using template D and 4 pieces using template Dr
(E6) 8 Diamonds using template E

Fabric #7: (F7) 1 – 13" Square - Cut in half twice diagonally to make four triangles.
(G7) 4 - 8 ⅝" Squares

Construction

1. To make the center octagon, sew an A1 triangle to an A2 triangle. Make 4. Then sew the four units together to make an octagon as shown. Press toward the red fabric. To reduce the bulk in the center, unpick a few stitches from each seam and coax the triangle points to form a circle.

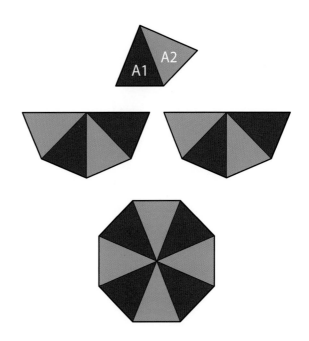

2. To make the octagon into a square, sew one B3 triangle to each of the A1 triangles. Press toward the light fabric.

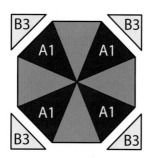

3. To make the feathered points, you need 56 half-square triangle units. Pair up an H4 triangle with an H5 triangle and sew them together on the diagonal. Chain-piece the triangles to make a total of 56 – 2" unfinished half-square triangle units.

4. To make a side unit, piece together four half-square triangle units using a scant ¼" seam allowance from step 3 plus one H5 triangle, as shown. Then sew together another three half-square triangle units again using a scant ¼" seam allowance and one H5 triangle as shown. Sew the strips to an F7 triangle using partial seams (sew only where indicated by the dark lines).

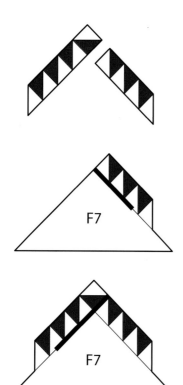

Sew one Dr6 piece to the side unit as shown. Join one D6 piece and one B3 triangle together; attach it to the unit as shown. Make four of these units.

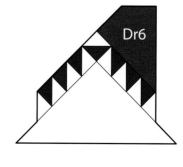

5. To make a corner unit, pair up eight H5 triangles and eight E6 diamonds. Sew them together to make eight units. Note: Four of these units will be the reverse of the other four as shown below.

Make a strip of four half-square triangle units and one unit from step 5 as shown. Now make another strip of three half-square triangle units and one unit from step 5 as shown. When making the strips for this step, use a scant ¼" seam allowance. Beginning with the smaller strip, sew them to a G7 square. Make four of these units.

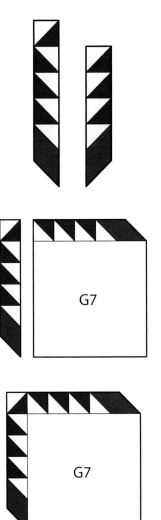

6. Join the center, four side units and four corner units as shown. Stitch the seams in the order indicated by the dark lines to complete the partial seams. Join the rows together in the same manner to complete the block.

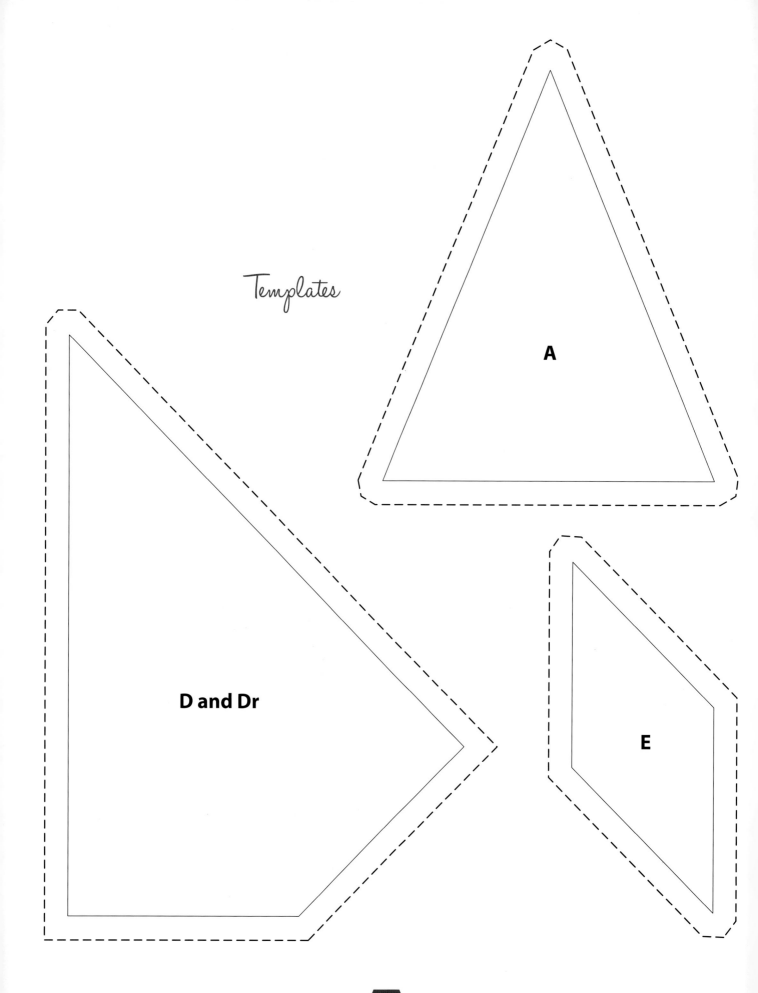

Templates

A

D and Dr

E

BLOCK SIZE: 28 ½" unfinished

Fabric Requirements

Fabric #1: 5" x WOF (red on white print)
Fabric #2: 8" x WOF (red print 1)
Fabric #3: 12" x WOF (white on white)
Fabric #4: 8" x WOF (red print 2)
Fabric #5: 10" x 10" (light red print)
Fabric #6: 14" square (white)
Fabric #7: 5" x 10" (white print 1)
Fabric #8: 5" x 10" (white print 2)

Cutting Instructions

Fabric #1: 2 – 2" x WOF Strip

Fabric #2: 2 – 2" x WOF Strip
1 – 2" x 15" Strip

Fabric #3: 2 – 2" x WOF Strip
1 – 2" x 15" Strip
1 – 2" x 13" Strip
(A3) 16 – Triangles using template A

Fabric #4: 2 – 2" x WOF Strip
1 – 2" x 15" Strip
1 – 2" x 13" Strip
1 – 2" x 12" Strip

Fabric #5: (B5) 8 – Triangles using template B

Fabric #6: (C6) 4 – 9" Squares
(D6) 1 – 13 1/2" Square - Cut in half twice diagonally to make four triangles.

Fabric #7: (B7) 4 – Triangles using template B

Fabric #8: (B8) 4 – Triangles using template B

Construction

For best results, lay out all the pieces you've cut according to the diagram before you sew.

1. Sew the 2" x WOF strips together in the order given. Stagger the strips by 1" as shown. Press toward fabric #2 and #4.

Note: If you do not stagger the strips, you will not have enough fabric. We recommend you starch the strips sets prior to cutting the diamonds. Starch helps reduce bias stretching on these units. Once cut, do not handle the diamonds units any more than necessary.

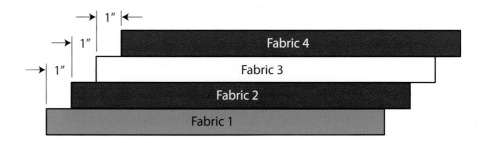

2. Use the 45-degree angle on your ruler to cut 2" wide strips. Cut eight 4-diamond strips like those shown below.

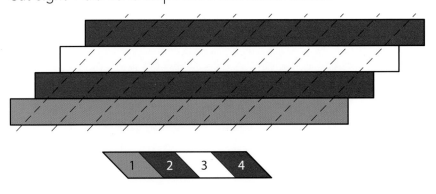

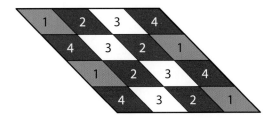

3. Sew four of the diamond strips together, alternating the position of fabric #1 as shown. Make two of these "A" points.

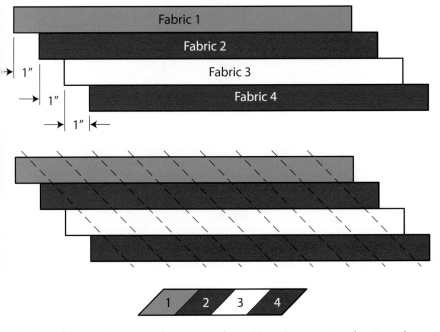

4. Sew 4 more strips together in the order shown below and cut them 2" wide at a 45-degree angle. Notice that these strips are cut in the opposite direction as the ones that were cut for the A points. Cut eight 4-diamond strips like the one shown below.

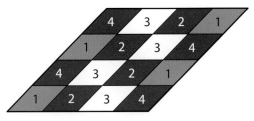

5. Sew four strips together to make a B point, again altering the position of fabric #1 as shown. Make two of these B points.

6. Make the following strip sets:

Strip Set 1
Sew together the 2" x 15" strips of fabric #2, #3 and #4 together in order. Stagger the strips by 1" as shown. Press towards the red fabrics. Use the 45-degree angle on your ruler to cut four 3-diamond strips.

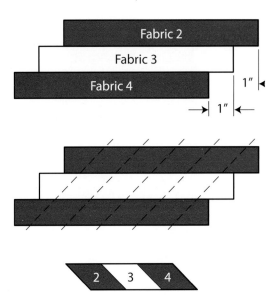

Sew an A3 triangle to the #4 end of each strip. Press toward the red fabric.

Strip Set 2
Sew together the 2" x 13" strips of fabric #3 and #4 together. Stagger the strips by 1" as shown. Press towards the red fabric. Use the 45-degree angle on your ruler to cut four 2-diamond strips.

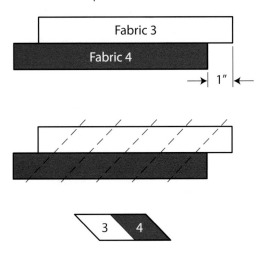

Sew an A3 triangle to the #4 end of each strip. Press toward the red fabric.

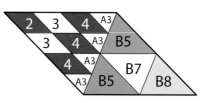

7. Use the 45-degree angle on your ruler to cut four diamonds from the 2" x 12" strip of fabric #4. Pair up four A3 triangles with the four diamonds and sew them together.

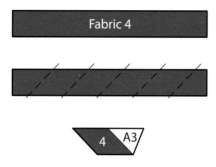

8. Draw ¼" seam lines on the wrong side of all the B triangles to help ensure accurate points.

9. Then sew a B5 triangle to either side of a B7 triangle as shown. Complete the unit by sewing a B8 triangle to the B7 triangle. Make four of these units.

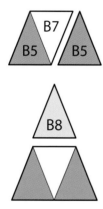

10. To make a diamond/triangle unit sew together: one 3-diamond strip, one 2-diamond strip, a 1-diamond/triangle unit and an A3 triangle, as shown. Then sew a unit from Step 9 to the A3 side of the pieced triangle as shown. Make four of these diamond/triangle units.

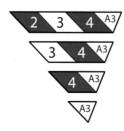

11. On the wrong side of the C6 squares and D6 triangles use a pencil to mark the ¼" point.

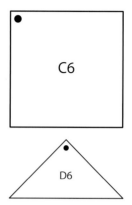

12. Pair up a unit from step 10 with an A diamond from step 3. Sew them together as shown. Make sure the diamond/triangle unit is always on the right side. Then, using an inset seam, add a C6 square to the corner. Make two of these A corner pieces.

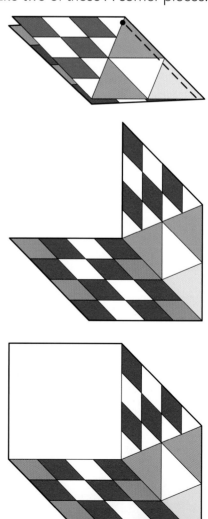

13. Repeat using the B point diamond from step 5 and make two B corner pieces.

14. Sew the four corner pieces together as shown, leaving a ¼" opening where indicated by the black dots.

15. Use an inset seam to add the D6 triangles. Always sew from the center outward. Trim as necessary to make the block 28 ½" square.

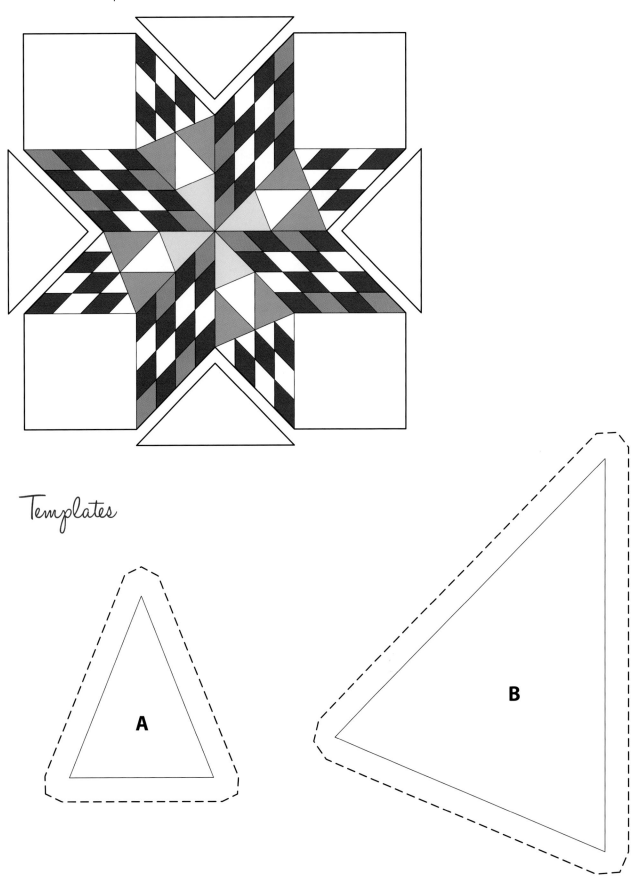

Templates

A

B

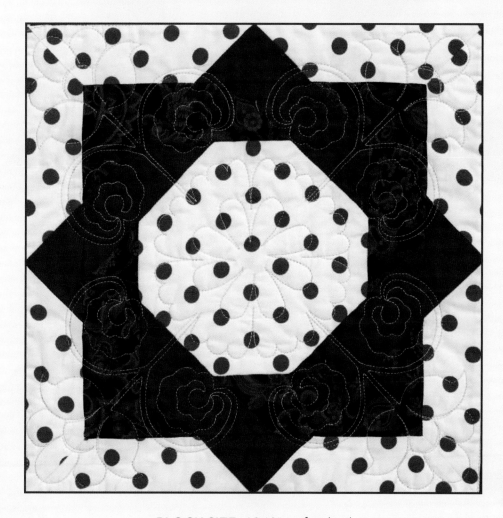

BLOCK SIZE: 12 ½" unfinished

Fabric Requirements

Fabric #1: 14" x 17" (polka dot)
Fabric #2: 7" x 14" (dark red print 1)
Fabric #3: 10" square (dark red print 2)

Cutting Instructions

Fabric #1: (A1) 1 – Octagon using template A
(F1) 8 – Pieces using template F
Fabric #2: (B2) 4 – Pieces using template B
(D2) 1 – 4 ³⁄₁₆" Square - Cut in half twice diagonally to make four triangles.
Fabric #3: (C3) 4 – Pieces using template C
(E3) 2 – 3 ⅞" Squares - Cut in half once diagonally to make four triangles.

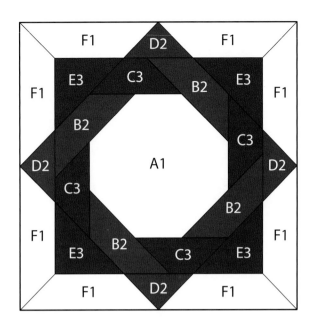

Construction

For best results, lay out all the pieces you've cut according to the diagram BEFORE you sew!

1. Note: The octagon has four short and four long sides. Read the instructions carefully. Sew a B2 piece to a long side of the A1 octagon with a partial seam, as indicated by the dark line.

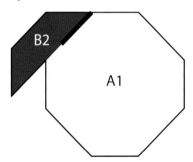

2. Add a C3 piece along the adjoining short side of the A1 octagon. Continue adding B2s and C3s alternately. After the last C3 is added, complete the partial seam as indicated by the dark line.

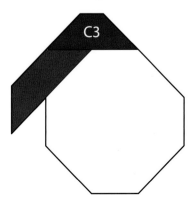

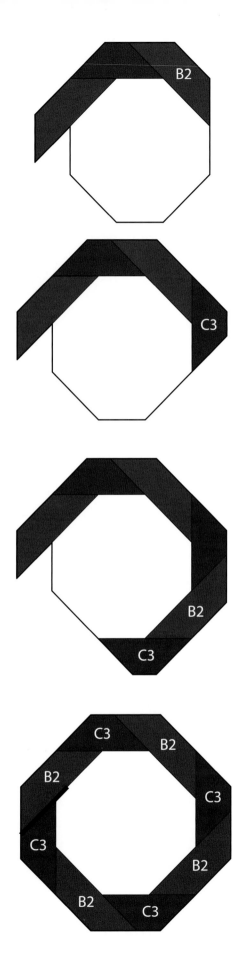

3. Sew a D2 triangle to each of the SHORT sides of the pieced octagon.

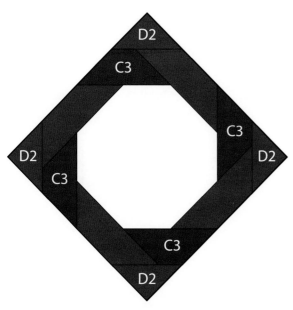

4. To make a corner, add two F1 pieces to one E3 triangle using an inset seam. Make three more identical corners.

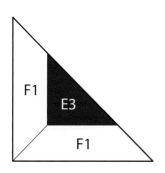

5. Sew two corners to opposite sides of the square. Then add the remaining sides. The block should measure 12 ½".

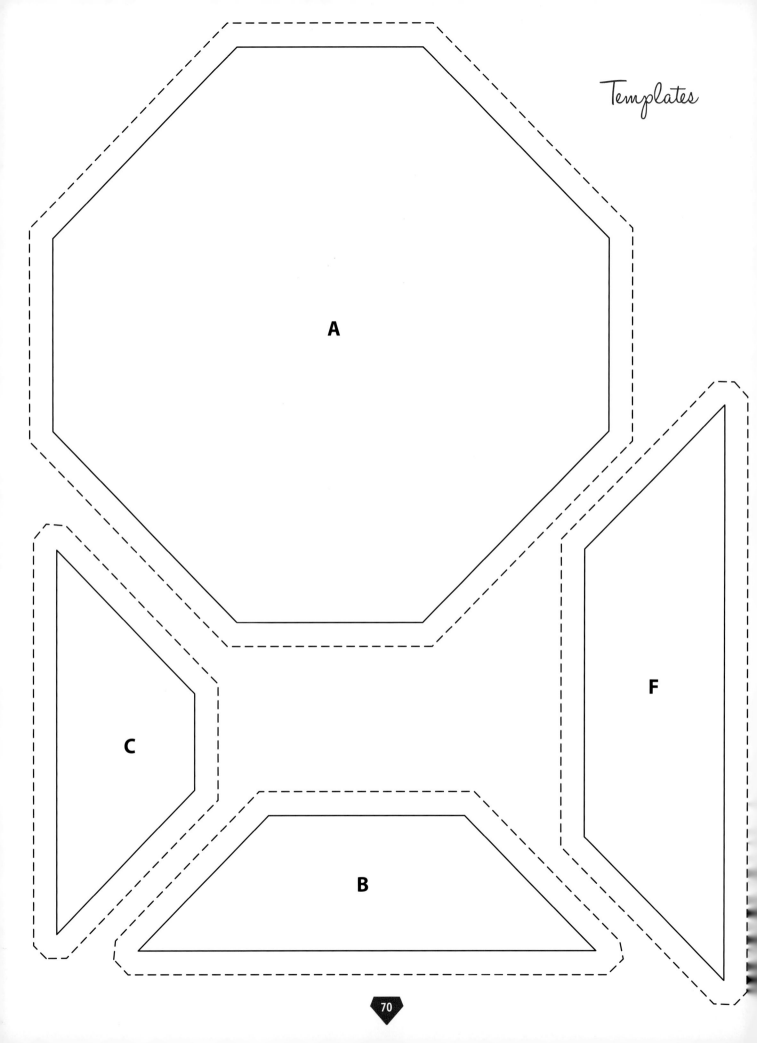

A

F

C

B

BLOCK SIZE: 12 ½" unfinished

Fabric Requirements

Fabric #1: 10" x 16" (dark red print)
Fabric #2: 12" x 16" (red print on white)
Fabric #3: 8" square (medium red print)
Fabric #4: 8" x 10" (red check)

Cutting Instructions

Fabric #1: (A1) 1 – 5 ⅛" Square - Cut in half once diagonally to make two triangles.
(B1) 2 – Triangles using template B
(C1) 2 – Triangles using template C

Fabric #2: (A2) 1 – 5 ⅛" Square - Cut in half once diagonally to make two triangles.
(D2) 4 – Triangles using template D

Fabric #3: (A3) 1 – 7 ¼" Square - Cut in half twice diagonally to make four triangles.

Fabric #4: (B4) 2 – Triangles using template B
(C4) 2 – Triangles using template C

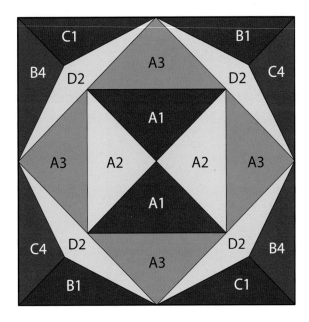

Construction

For best results, lay out all the pieces you've cut according to the diagram BEFORE you sew!

1. To make the hourglass center, sew an A1 triangle to an A2 triangle along the short side. Make two identical units and join them to make a square.

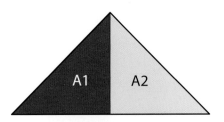

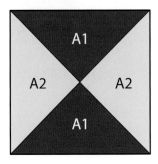

2. Next, sew two A3 triangles to opposite sides of the hourglass square. Then add the remaining A3 triangles. At this point, the block should measure 9" unfinished.

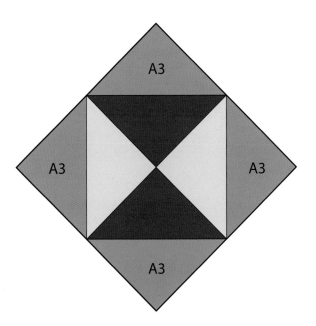

3. The corners are made with an inset seam. Mark the ¼" intersection at the top of the wrong side of the B1 and B4 triangles. With right sides together, place a B1 triangle on top of a C4 triangle and stitch along the short sides, beginning at the ¼" mark. Press the seam open. Make two C4/B1 units and two C1/B4 units.

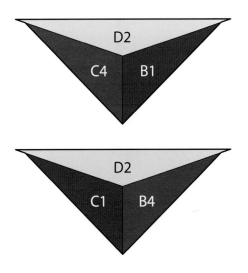

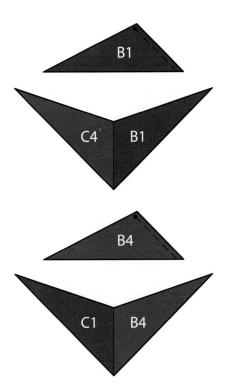

4. Sew two corner units to opposite sides of the block as shown. Then add the remaining corner units. The block should measure 12 ½".

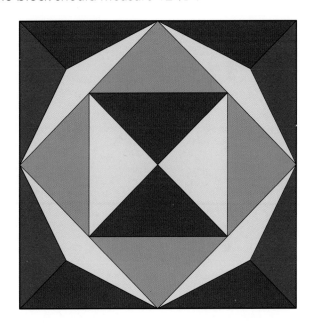

Mark the ¼" intersection at the top of the wrong side of the D2 triangles. With right sides together, place a D2 triangle on top of a B1 triangle and stitch as shown, starting at the ¼" mark. Now sew the other edge of the D2 triangle to a C4 triangle – again starting at the ¼" mark. Complete the other three corners units the same way.

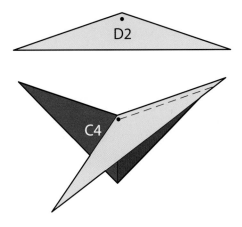

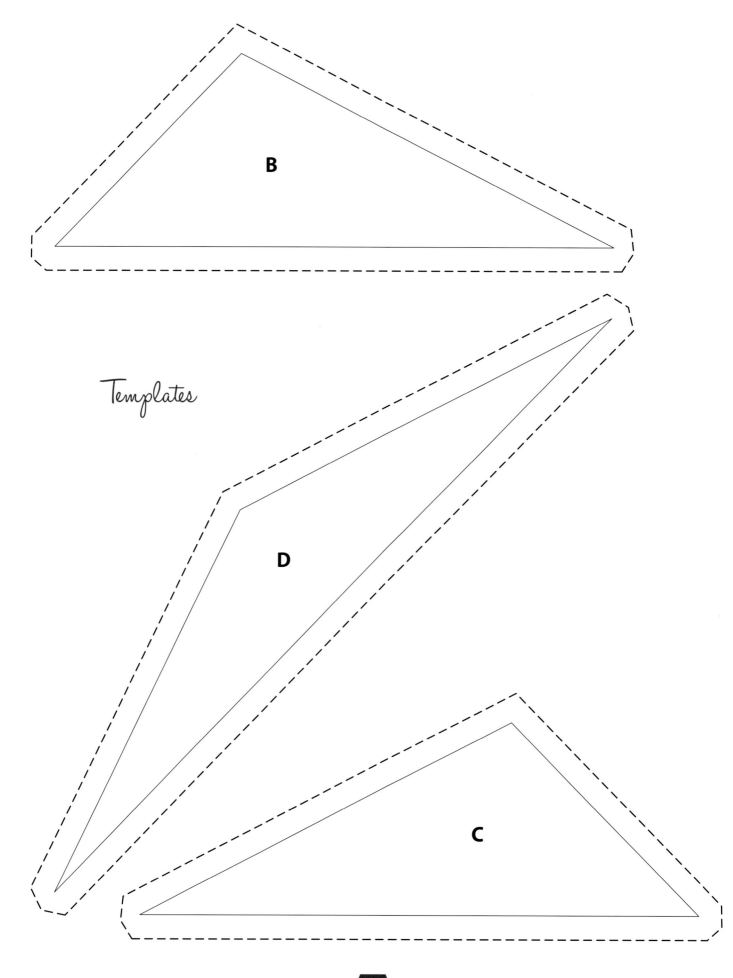

Templates

B

D

C

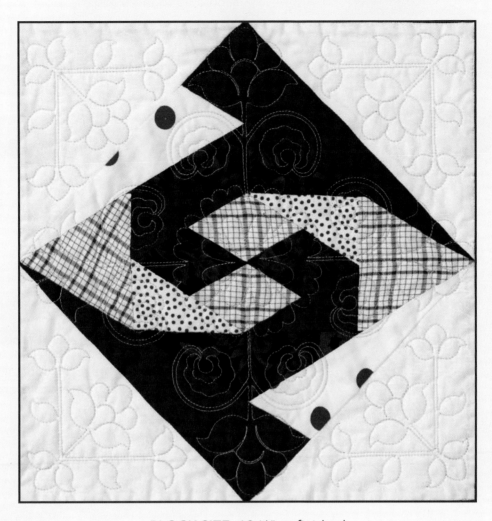

BLOCK SIZE: 12 ½" unfinished

Fabric Requirements

Fabric #1: 6" x 12" (dark red print 1)
Fabric #2: 5" x 11" (plaid)
Fabric #3: 4" x 16" (dark red print 2)
Fabric #4: 3" x 5" (red on white print 1)
Fabric #5: 5" x 10" (red on white print 2)
Fabric #6: 8" x 15" (white)

Cutting Instructions

Fabric #1: (A1) 2 – Diamonds using template A
(C1) 2 – Triangles using template C
Fabric #2: (A2) 2 – Diamonds using template A
(D2) 2 – Triangles using template D
Fabric #3: (B3) 2 – Triangles using template B
(F3) 2 – Triangles using template F
Fabric #4: (Br4) 2 – Triangles using template Br
Fabric #5: (E5) 2 – Triangles using template E
Fabric #6: (G6) 2 – 6 ⅞" Squares - Cut in half once
diagonally to make four triangles.

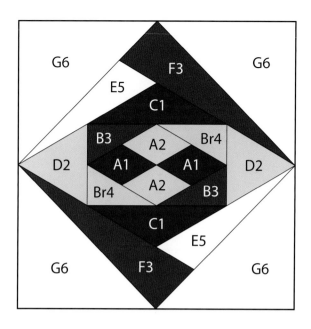

Construction

For best results, lay out all the pieces you've cut according to the diagram before you sew.

1. To make the center of the block, pair up the A1 and A2 diamonds. Sew them together as shown and press toward the red. Join the pairs together and press to one side.

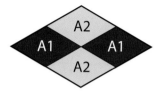

2. Add the B3 triangles to opposite sides of the center diamonds. Then add the Br4 triangles to the remaining sides.

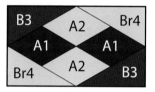

3. Sew the C1 triangles to the long sides of the block. Now sew the D2 triangles to the short sides of the block.

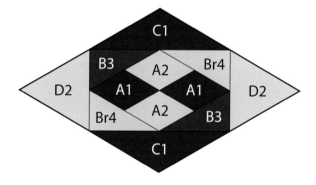

4. Sew the E5 triangles to the top left and bottom right sides of the block. Then add the F3 triangles to the other two sides.

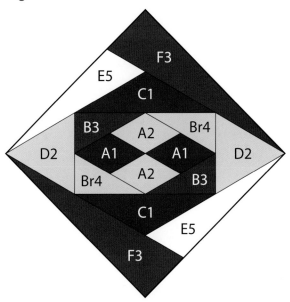

5. Sew a G6 triangle to each side of the block. The block should measure 12 ½".

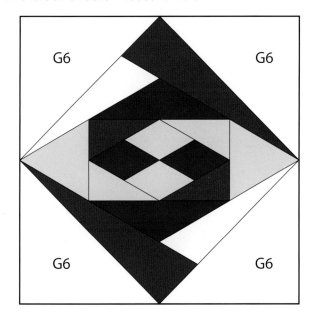

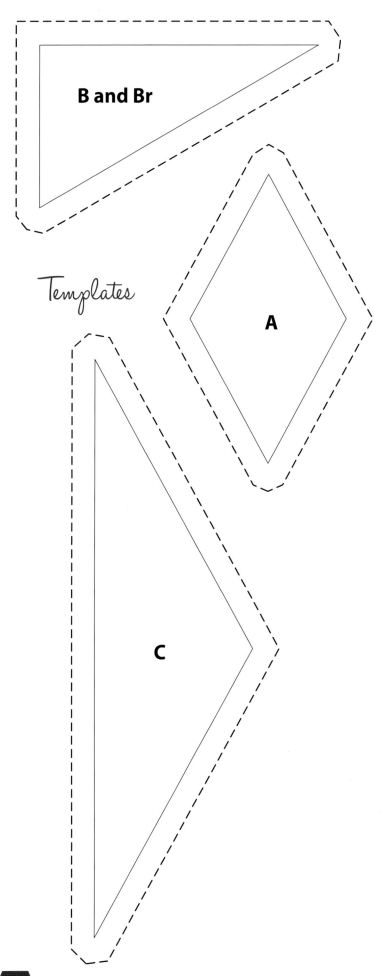

Templates

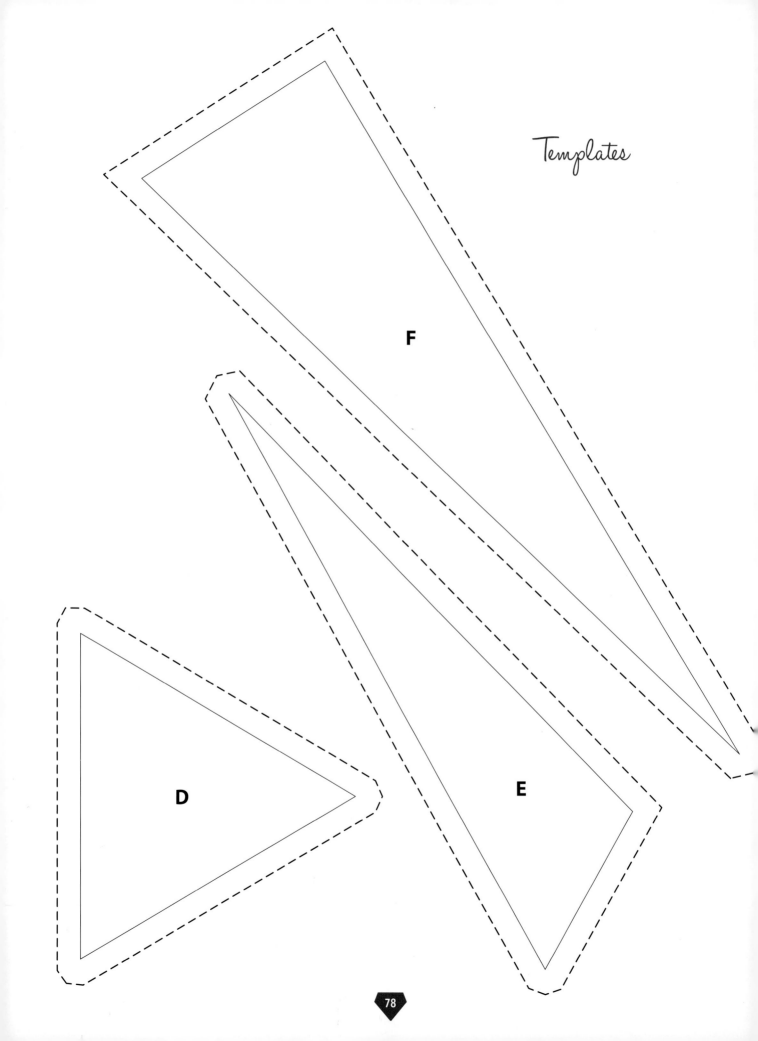

Templates

F

E

D

BLOCK SIZE: 12 ½" unfinished

Fabric Requirements

Fabric #1: 7" x 15" (large red print)
Fabric #2: 7" x 10" (white)
Fabric #3: 7" x 15" (red print on white)
Fabric #4: 7" x 10" (red print)
Fabric #5: 8" x 10" (red print on cream)

Cutting Instructions

Fabric #1: (A1) 1 – 1 ⅞" Square - Cut in half once diagonally to make two triangles.
(C1) 2 – Pieces using template C
(E1) 2 – Pieces using template E
(G1) 1 – 5 ⅞" Square - Cut in half once diagonally to make two triangles.

Fabric #2: (B2) 2 – Pieces using template B
(D2) 2 – Pieces using template D
(F2) 2 – Pieces using template F

Fabric #3: (A3) 1 – 1 ⅞" Square - Cut in half once diagonally to make two triangles.
(C3) 2 – Pieces using template C
(E3) 2 – Pieces using template E
(G3) 1 – 5 ⅞" Square - Cut in half once diagonally to make two triangles.

Fabric #4: (B4) 2 – Pieces using template B
(D4) 2 – Pieces using template D
(F4) 2 – Pieces using template F

Fabric #5: (H5) 8 – Pieces using template H

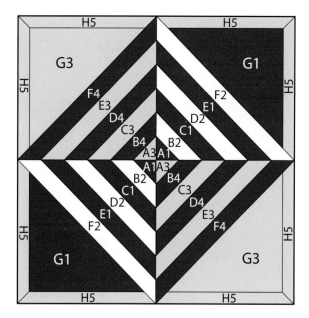

Construction

For best results, lay out all the pieces you've cut according to the diagram before you sew.

1. Pair up an A1 triangle and a B2 piece and sew them together. Then add a C1, D2, E1 and F2 as shown. Press toward the reds. Make two units.

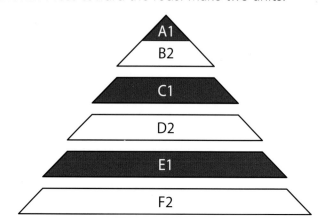

2. Mark the ¼" points on the reverse side of the H5 pieces. Sew two H5 pieces to a G1 triangle to make a corner unit. You will need to miter the corner so stop sewing at the quarter-inch mark. Close the mitered seam by sewing outward from the marked dot to the outer edge. Make two units. Then, sew a corner unit to an F2 striped unit from Step 1 and press toward the red. The square should measure 6 ½" unfinished. Make two.

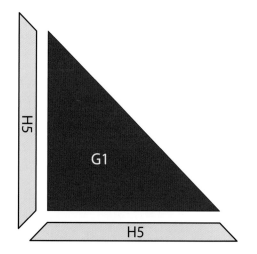

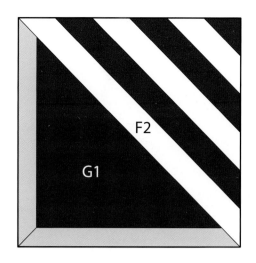

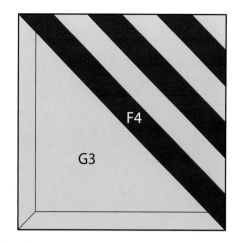

5. Sew the four squares together as shown. The block should measure 12 ½".

3. Pair up an A3 triangle and a B4 piece and sew them together. Then add a C3, D4, E3 and F4 as shown. Press toward the reds. Make two units.

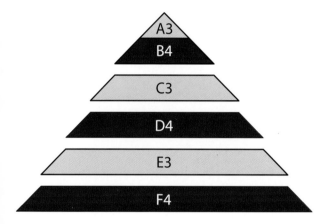

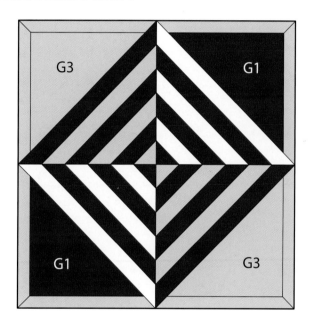

4. Follow the directions in step 2 and sew two H5 strips to a G3 triangle to make a corner unit. Make two. Then, sew a corner unit to an F4 striped unit from Step 3 and press toward the red. The square should measure 6 ½". Make two.

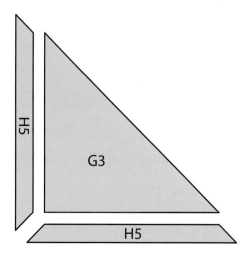

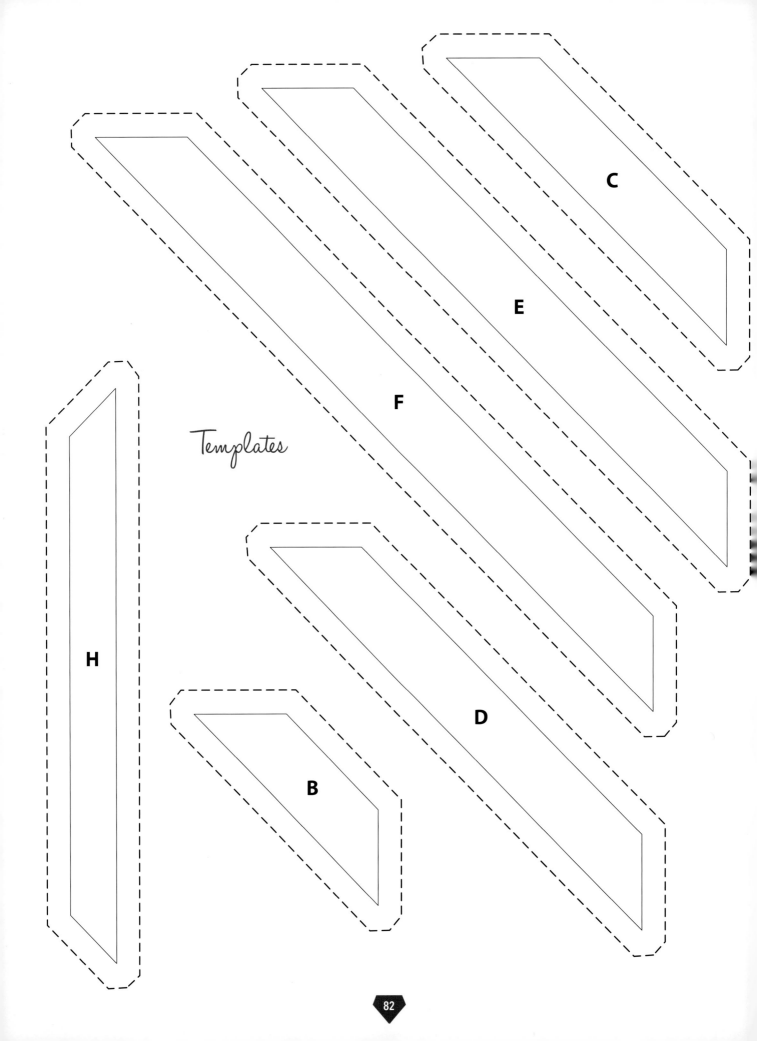

C

E

F

Templates

H

D

B

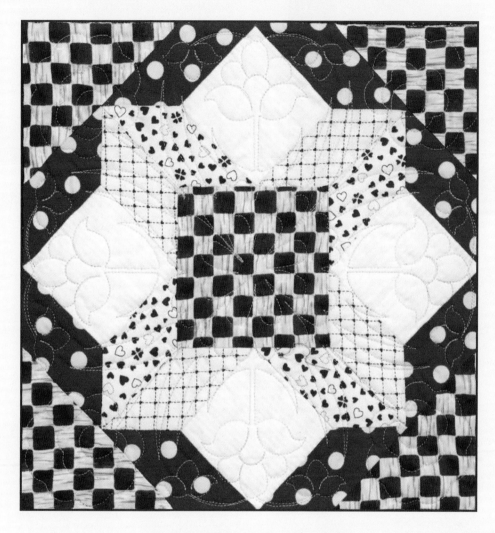

BLOCK SIZE: 12 ½" unfinished

Fabric Requirements

Fabric #1: 6" x 16" (checks)
Fabric #2: 8" x 8" (white)
Fabric #3: 6" x 10" (red print on white 1)
Fabric #4: 6" x 10" (red print on white 2)
Fabric #5: 6" x 20" (white on red print)

Cutting Instructions

Fabric #1: (A1) 1 – 4 ½" Square
(E1) 2 – 4 ⅞" Squares - Cut in half once diagonally to make four triangles.
Fabric #2: (B2) 4 – 3 ⅜" Squares
Fabric #3: (C3) 4 – Diamonds using template C
Fabric #4: (D4) 4 – Diamonds using template D
Fabric #5: (C5) 4 – Diamonds using template C
(D5) 4 – Diamonds using template D

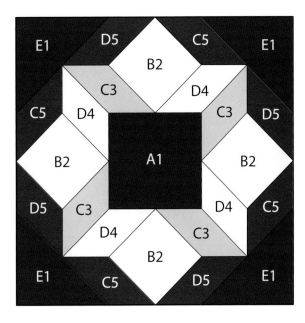

Construction

For best results, lay out all the pieces you've cut according to the diagram BEFORE you sew!

1. Draw ¼" seam lines on the wrong side of all B squares and C and D diamonds to ensure accurate points.

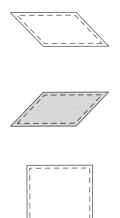

2. To make a side unit, sew one C3 diamond to the B square, stopping at the ¼" mark. Press the seam toward the diamond. Then sew one D4 diamond next to the C3 diamond, again starting at the ¼" mark. Press the seam toward the diamond.

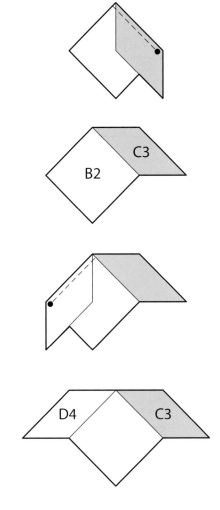

3. Sew one C5 diamond and one D5 diamond using inset seams to the remaining sides of the B2 square. Make four of these side units.

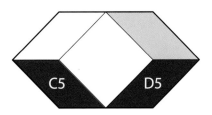

4. To add one side unit to the center square, position the C3 diamond and D4 diamond next to the square. Sew the side unit to the square, starting and stopping at the ¼" mark. Press the seam toward the square. Add the remaining side units using inset seams.

5. Sew one E1 triangle to each corner to complete the block.

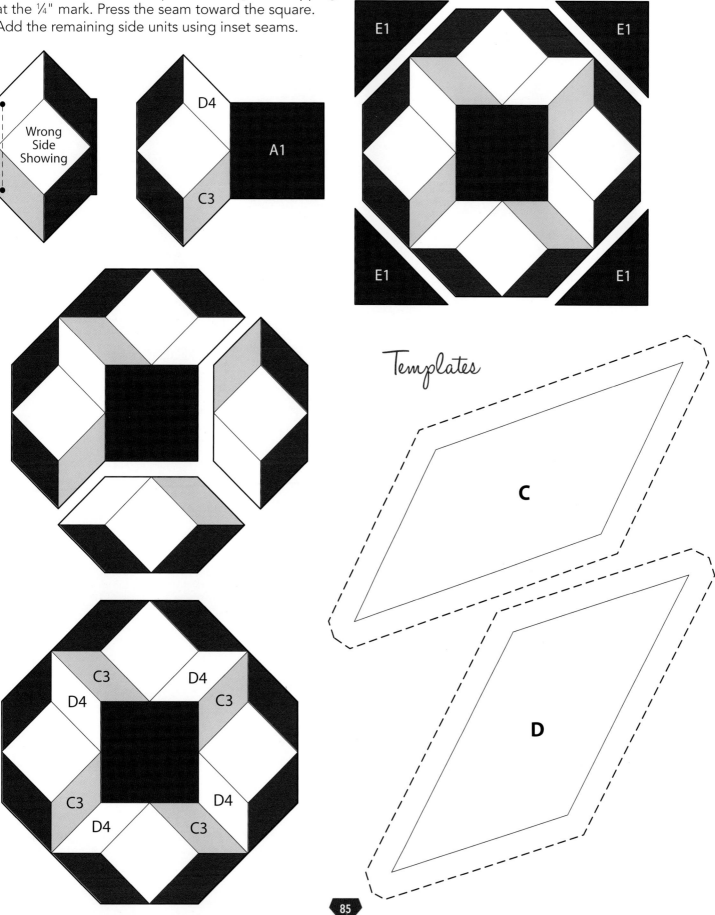

Templates

BLOCK SIZE: 12 ½" unfinished

Fabric Requirements

Fabric #1: 12" square (white print 1)
Fabric #2: 5" x 10" (red print 1)
Fabric #3: 5" x 10" (red print 2)
Fabric #4: 12" square (white print 2)
Fabric #5: 5" x 10" (red print 3)
Fabric #6: 5" x 10" (red print 4)

Cutting Instructions

Fabric #1: (A1) 8 – Triangles using template A
(B1) 8 – Triangles using template B
(D1) 4 – 2 ⅜" Squares - Cut in half once diagonally to make eight triangles.
Fabric #2: (C2) 4 – Triangles using template C
Fabric #3: (C3) 4 – Triangles using template C
Fabric #4: (A4) 8 – Triangles using template A
(B4) 8 – Triangles using template B
(D4) 4 – 2 ⅜" Squares - Cut in half once diagonally to make eight triangles.
Fabric #5: (C5) 4 – Triangles using template C
Fabric #6: (C6) 4 – Triangles using template C

Construction

For best results, lay out all the pieces you've cut according to the diagram before you sew.

1. Pair up four A1 and C2 triangles as shown below. Sew them together and press toward the red.

2. Add one B1 triangle to each unit as shown and press toward the red.

3. Sew one D1 triangle to the corner of each unit and press toward the white.

4. Sew the four squares together as shown. To reduce bulk in the center, unpick a few stitches from each seam and coax the triangle points to form a circle.

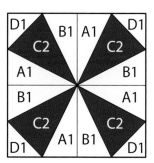

5. Repeat steps 1 – 4 to make three more units. Use the following fabric combinations to complete the four square units: fabrics #1 white and #3 red, fabrics #4 white and #5 red, fabrics #4 white and #6 red. When you have all four units finished, sew them together as shown. The block should measure 12 ½".

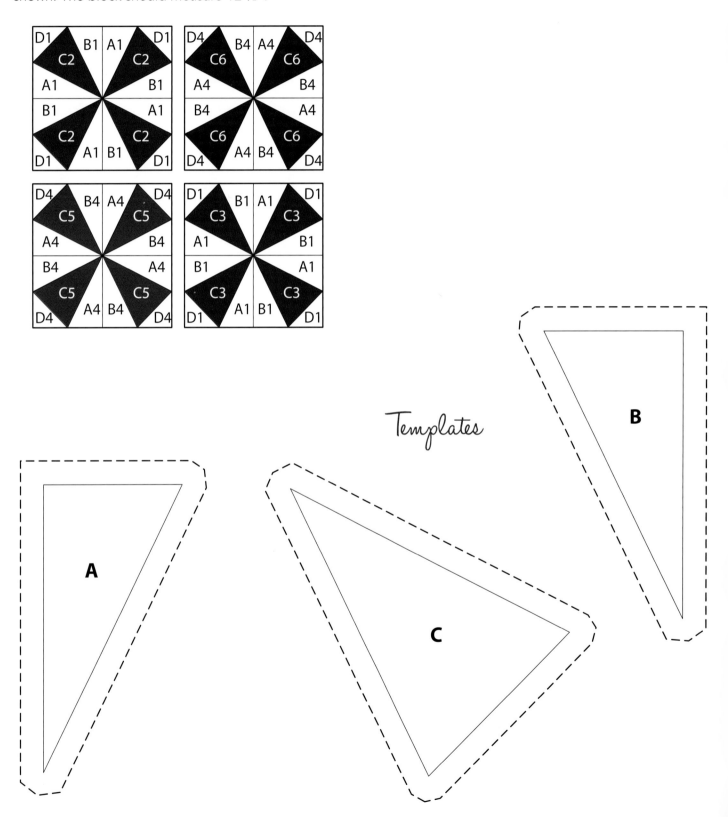

Templates

BLOCK 22 – *Marquise*

BLOCK SIZE: 12 ½" unfinished

Fabric Requirements

Fabric #1: 10" x 26" (white)
Fabric #2: 6" x 14" (red print 1)
Fabric #3: 6" x 14" (red print 2)

Cutting Instructions

Fabric #1: (A1) 16 – Triangles using template A
(B1) 16 – Triangles using template B
Fabric #2: (C2) 4 – Strips using template C
(D2) 4 – Strips using template D
Fabric #3: (C3) 4 – Strips using template C
(D3) 4 – Strips using template D

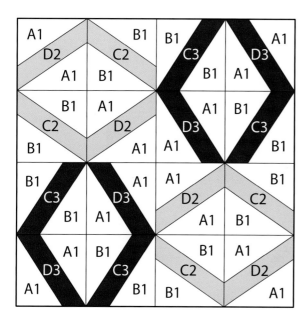

4. Repeat Steps 1 – 3 using fabric #1 and fabric #3. Then sew the four units together to complete the block as shown. The block should measure 12 ½".

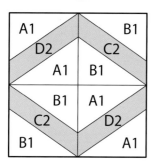

Construction

For best results, lay out all the pieces you've cut according to the diagram before you sew.

1. Sew an A1 triangle to either side of a D2 strip as shown below. The unit should measure 3 ½". Make 4 units.

2. Sew a B1 triangle to either side of a C2 strip as shown below. The unit should measure 3 ½". Make 4 units.

3. Arrange the units from step 1 and step 2 as shown below and sew them together. This four-patch should measure 6 ½". Make 2 units.

Templates

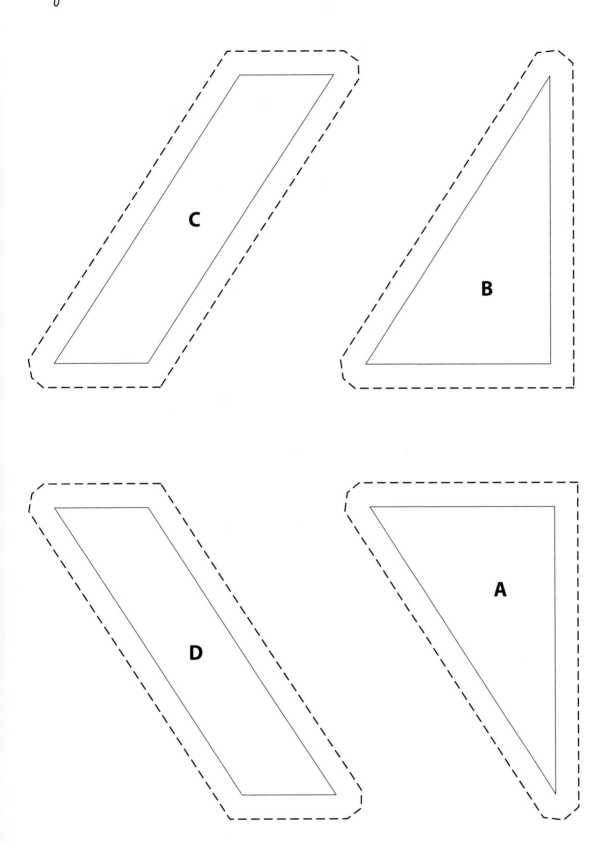

C

B

D

A

BLOCK SIZE: 12 ½" unfinished

Fabric Requirements

Fabric #1: 7" x 27" (large red print)
Fabric #2: 7" x 27" (small red print on white)
Fabric #3: 7" square (dark red)

Cutting Instructions

Fabric #1: (A1) 1 – 6 ½" Square
(B1) 4 – Diamonds using template B
(C1) 4 – Diamonds using template C
Fabric #2: (B2) 4 – Diamonds using template B
(C2) 4 – Diamonds using template C
(E2) 2 – 3 ⅞" Squares - Cut in half once diagonally to make four triangles.
Fabric #3: (D3) 4 – 2 ⅝" Squares

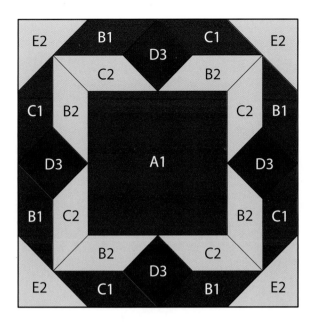

Construction

For best results, lay out all the pieces you've cut according to the diagram BEFORE you sew!

1. Draw ¼" seam lines on the wrong side of all B2 and C2 diamonds, the A1 square and all the D3 squares to help ensure accuracy.

2. Pair up the B1 and C2 diamonds. Sew them together leaving the ¼" seam allowance open at the top as shown. Then pair up all the B2 and C1 diamonds and sew them together the same way.

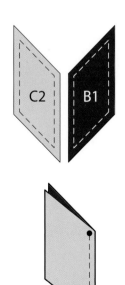

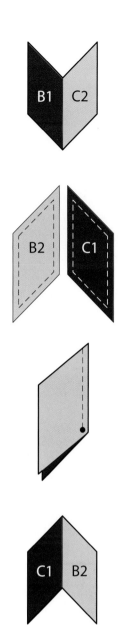

3. To make the side units, pair up each D3 square to a B1/C2 unit. Sew the square to the unit with an inset seam. Then add a C1/B2 unit to the remaining side of each D3 square. You should have four side units.

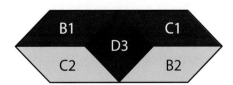

4. Sew two side units to opposite sides of the A1 square, starting and stopping at the ¼" point on each corner. Be sure to have fabric #2 on each side of the A1 square. Then add side units to the remaining sides of the A1 square in the same manner. Sew the four side openings together as indicated by the dark lines.

5. Sew an E2 triangle to each corner of the block. The block should measure 12 ½".

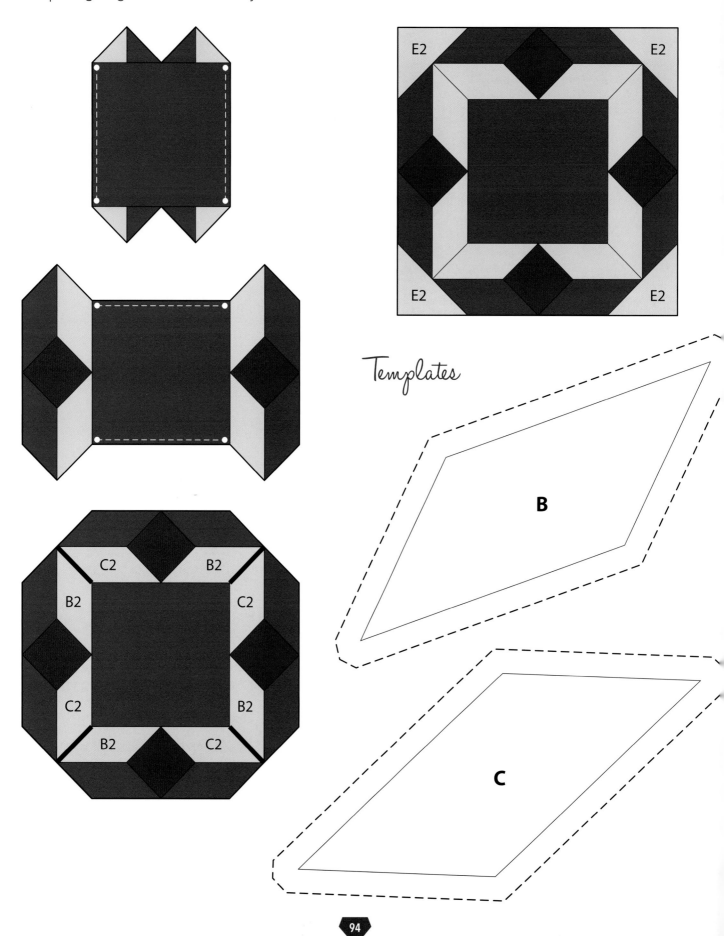

Templates

B

C

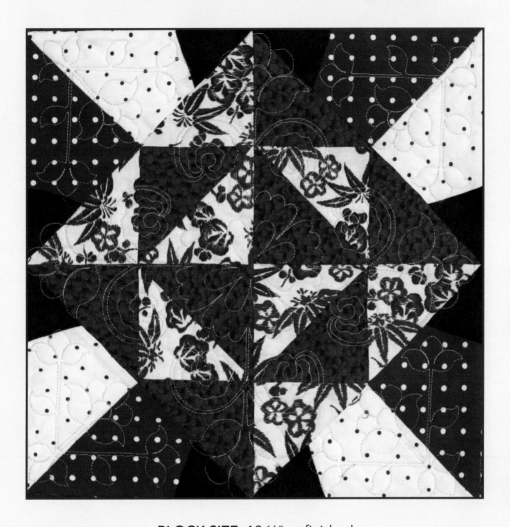

BLOCK SIZE: 12 ½" unfinished

Fabric Requirements

Fabric #1: 5" x 17" (red print on white 1)
Fabric #2: 5" x 17" (red print)
Fabric #3: 6" x 16" (red print on white 2)
Fabric #4: 6" x 16" (white print on red)
Fabric #5: 4" x 20" (dark red)

Cutting Instructions

Fabric #1: (A1) 4 – 3 ⅞" Squares - Cut in half once diagonally to make eight triangles.
Fabric #2: (A2) 4 – 3 ⅞" Squares - Cut in half once diagonally to make eight triangles.
Fabric #3: (B3) 4 – Pieces using template B
Fabric #4: (C4) 4 – Pieces using template C
Fabric #5: (D5) 4 – Triangles using template D
(E5) 4 – Triangles using template E

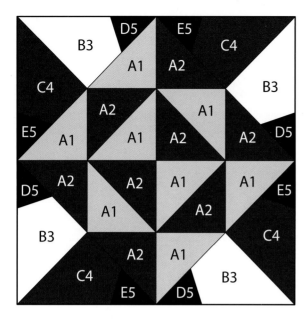

Construction

For best results, lay out all the pieces you've cut according to the diagram before you sew.

1. Pair up four A1 and A2 triangles. Sew them together to make four half-square triangle units. Sew the four HST units together as shown below. The square should measure 6 ½" unfinished.

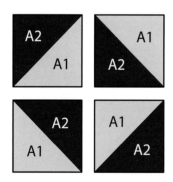

2. Pair up the remaining A1 and A2 triangles. Sew them together to make four corner triangle units. Note: Two units will have the light triangle on the left and two will have the light triangle on the right.

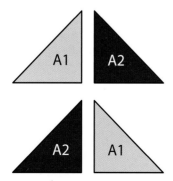

3. Sew two triangle units from step 2 to opposite sides of the square. Make sure the light triangles are always against the dark triangles. Sew the other two triangle units to the remaining sides of the square. The square should measure 9" unfinished.

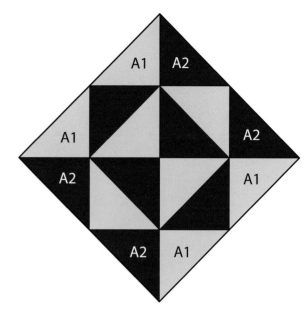

4. To make the corner units, pair up the B3 and C4 pieces and sew them together. Then add a D5 and E5 triangle to each end. Make four corner units.

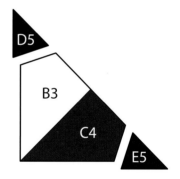

5. Sew two corner units to opposite sides of the square. Then add the other two corner units to the remaining sides of the square. The block should measure 12 ½".

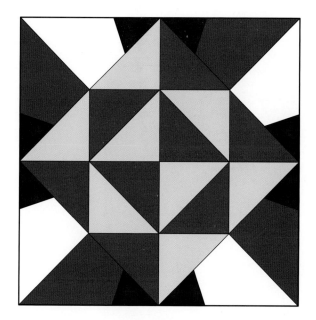

Templates

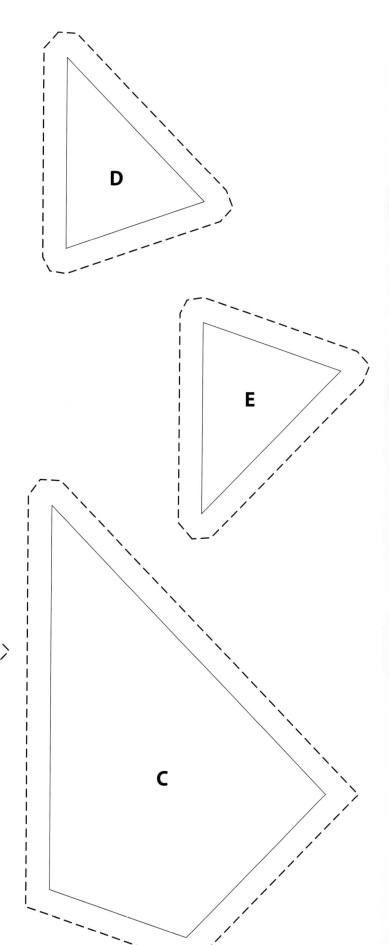

BLOCK SIZE: 12 ½" unfinished

Fabric Requirements

Fabric #1: 10" x 16" (red print on white)
Fabric #2: 8" x 20" (dark red print)
Fabric #3: 8" x 20" (medium red print)

Cutting Instructions

Fabric #1: (A1) 4 – Diamonds using template A
Fabric #2: (B2) 8 – Triangles using template B
Fabric #3: (C3) 8 – Triangles using template C

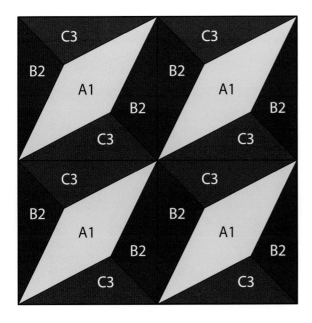

2. This block is a four-patch. To start one patch, sew both B2 triangles to opposite sides of the A1 diamond. Begin sewing at the ¼" marks.

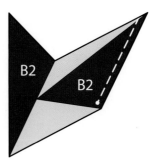

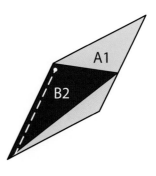

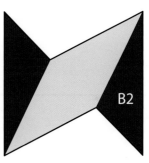

Construction

For best results, lay out all the pieces you've cut according to the diagram before you sew.

1. Mark the ¼" points at the top point on the wrong side of the B2 triangles and the C3 triangles as well as the sides of the A1 diamonds.

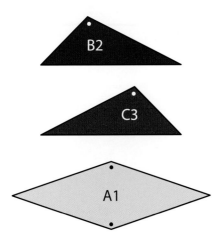

3. Next, add the C3 triangles using inset seams. The square should measure 6 ½" unfinished. Make four squares.

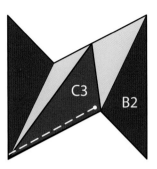

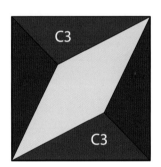

4. To assemble the blocks, you may want to try out different layouts. Choose your favorite cut …

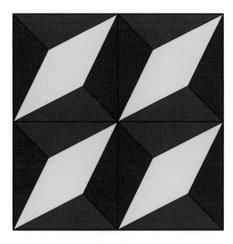

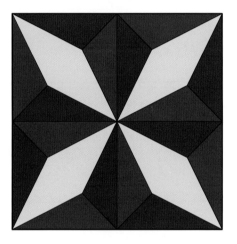

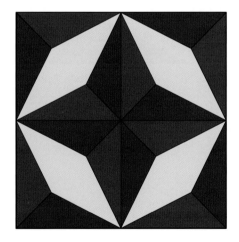

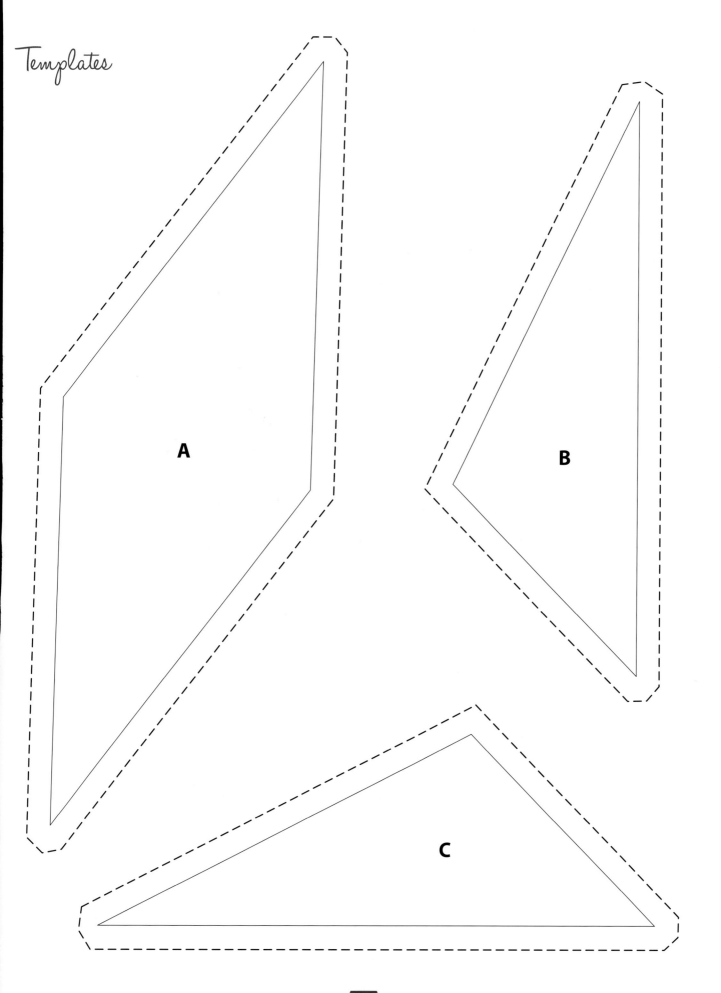

Templates

A

B

C

BLOCK SIZE: 12 ½" unfinished

Fabric Requirements

Fabric #1: 4" x 4" (dark red)
Fabric #2: 8" x 20" (red print 1)
Fabric #3: 8" x 20" (white)
Fabric #4: 8" x 14" (red print 2)

Cutting Instructions

Fabric #1: (A1) 1 – 2 ⅝" Square
Fabric #2: (B2) 2 – Pieces using template B
           (C2) 2 – Triangles using template C
           (D2) 2 – Triangles using template D
           (E2) 2 – Triangles using template E
Fabric #3: (B3) 2 – Pieces using template B
           (C3) 2 – Triangles using template C
           (D3) 2 – Triangles using template D
           (E3) 2 – Triangles using template E
Fabric #4: (F4) 4 – Pieces using template F
Note: The C and D templates are slightly different.

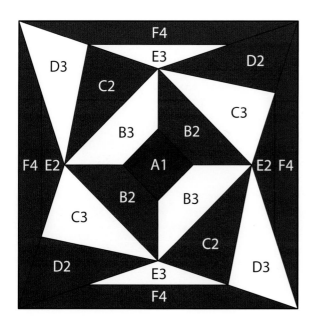

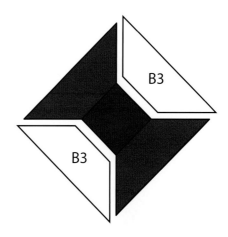

3. To make the corner points, pair up the C2 triangles with the D3 triangles and the C3 triangles with the D2 triangles. Sew them together into four triangle units.

Construction

For best results, lay out all the pieces you've cut according to the diagram before you sew.

1. Mark the ¼" points on the wrong side of all the B, C, D, and E pieces.

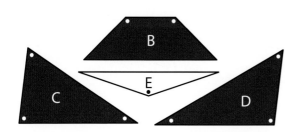

2. To make the center square, sew the B2 pieces to opposite sides of the A1 square. Start and stop at the ¼" marks. Then attach the B3 pieces using inset seams. The square should measure 6" unfinished.

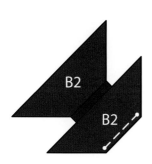

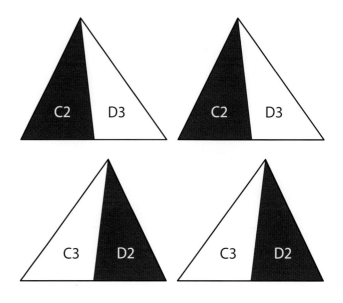

4. To make the side triangles, sew together an E2 triangle to an F4 piece. Make 2 units. Then sew together an E3 triangle to an F4 piece. Make 2 of these units.

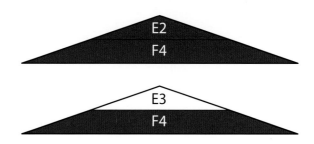

5. To attach the corner points to the square, sew the C2/D3 triangle units to the B3 sides. Next sew the C3/D2 units to the remaining sides. Finally, the side triangle units are added using inset seams. Make sure the E3/F4 units are attached to the "red sides" as shown.

Templates

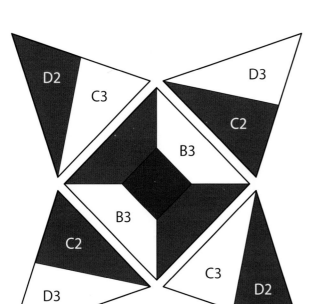

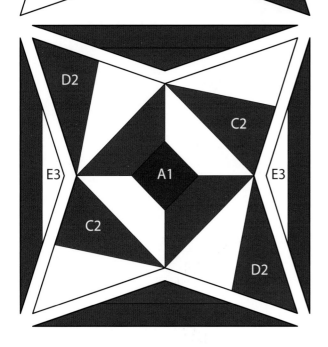

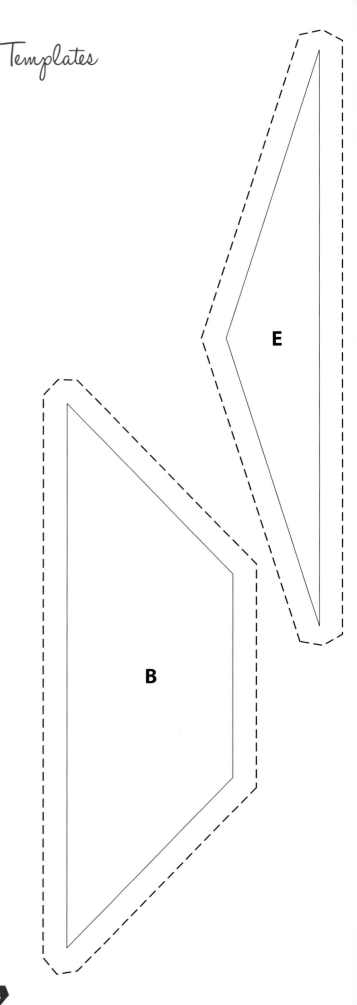

E

B

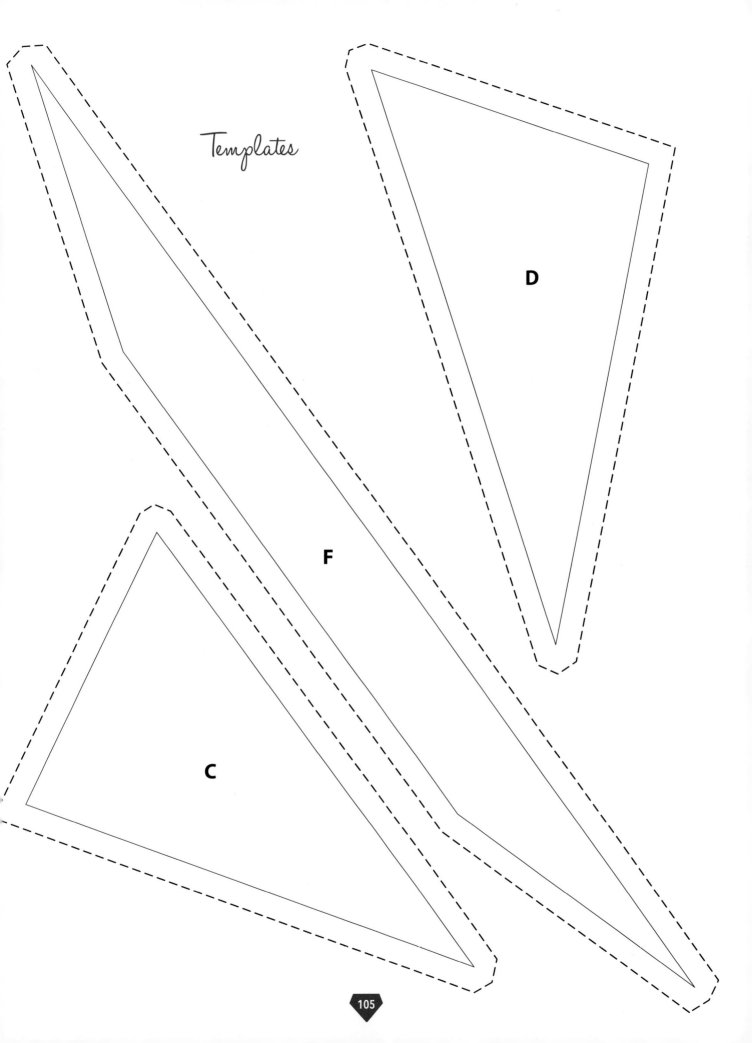

Templates

D

F

C

BLOCK 27 – *Be Mine*

BLOCK SIZE: 12 ½" unfinished

Fabric Requirements

Fabric #1: 8" x 20" (white)
Fabric #2: 8" x 13" (white print on red)
Fabric #3: 5" x 7" (red print 1)
Fabric #4: 5" x 7" (red print 2)
Fabric #5: 5" x 18" (dark red print)

Cutting Instructions

Fabric #1: (A1) 1 – Piece using template A
(I1) 2 – 6 ⅞" Squares - Cut in half once diagonally to make four triangles.
(J1) 2 – Pieces using template J
Fabric #2: (B2) 2 – Pieces using template B
(H2) 1 – 3 ⅛" Square - Cut in half once diagonally to make two triangles.
(K2) 2 Pieces using template K
Fabric #3: (C3) 2 – Pieces using template C
Fabric #4: (D4) 2 – Pieces using template D
Fabric #5: (E5) 2 – Pieces using template E
(F5) 2 – Pieces using template F
(G5) 2 – Pieces using template G

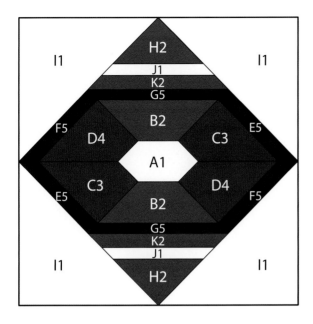

Construction

For best results, lay out all the pieces you've cut according to the diagram before you sew.

1. Mark the ¼" points at the top point on the wrong side of all the fabric pieces cut from templates.

2. Sew a C3 and a D4 piece to the A1 piece, starting and stopping at the 1/4" marks. Then attach a B2 piece using an inset seam.

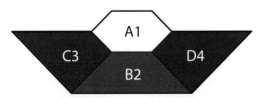

3. Sew the remaining C3 and D4 pieces to the unit. Now add the remaining B2 piece.

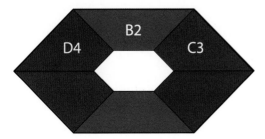

4. Next, sew an E5 and an F5 piece to the unit as shown. Then attach a G5 piece.

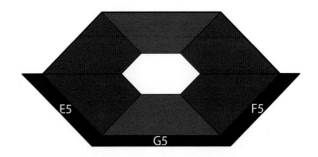

5. Sew the remaining E5 and F5 pieces to the unit. Now add the remaining G5 piece. Set unit aside.

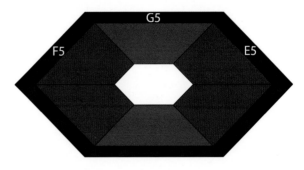

6. Sew a J1 piece to the bottom of an H2 triangle. Now add a K2 to the bottom. Make two of these units.

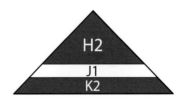

7. Sew the H2 units from Step 6 to the top and bottom of the unit from Step 5. Add the four I1 triangles to the corners.

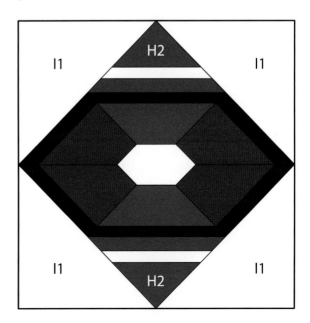

Templates

A

B

G

C

D

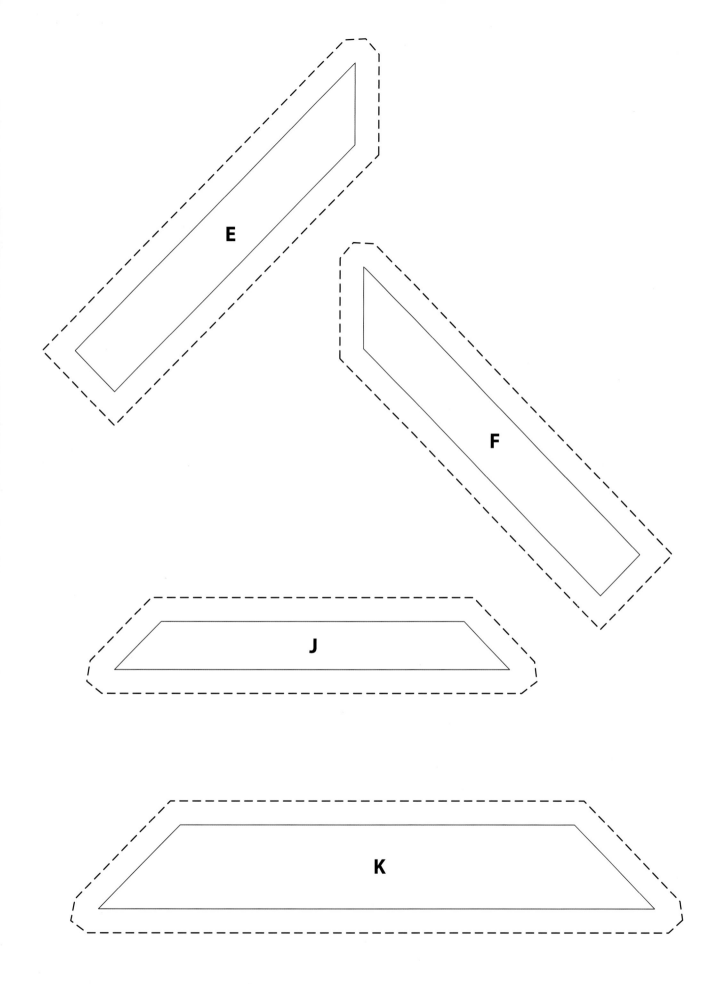

E

F

J

K

Finishing Instructions

FINAL SIZE: 100" x 100"

While the directions for making the sashing strips and corner posts remain the same as those used in Version 1 of the quilt, the fabric requirements change as well as the amount of pieces to cut. Refer to pages 49 and 50 for construction directions and page 55 for fabric requirements.

Sashing Strips

Cutting Instructions

Fabric #1: Cut 42 – 1 ⅞" strips. Cut the strips into 864 – 1 ⅞" squares. Cut each square in half once diagonally to make 1,728 triangles.

Fabric #2: Cut 42 – 1 ⅞" strips. Cut the strips into 864 – 1 ⅞" squares. Cut each square in half once diagonally to make 1,728 triangles.

Fabric #3: 72 – 2 ½" x 12 ½" rectangles

Construction

Pair up a fabric #1 with a fabric #2 triangle and sew together on the diagonal. Chain-piece the triangles to make a total of 1,728 – 1 ½" unfinished half-square triangle units.

Refer to the instructions on page 49 for directions and make 72 units.

Posts

Cutting Instructions

Fabric #1: (Al) 23 – 3 ¼" squares. Cut in half twice diagonally to make 92 triangles.
Fabric #2: (A2) 23 – 3 ¼" squares. Cut in half twice diagonally to make 92 triangles.
Fabric #3: (B3) 92 – 2 ½" x 1 ½" rectangles
Fabric #4: (C4) 92 – 4 ½" x 1 ½" rectangles

Refer to Posts Construction on page 50 to make 46 units.

Construction

1. We recommended you lay out the entire quilt before sewing everything together. The sashing strips are directional due to the half-square triangle placement, and you should orient them in a manner you find most visually appealing.

2. To begin, start by sewing the long sashing rows together. Sew seven posts and six sashing strips together as shown in the diagram. Make four.

3. Next sew the short sashing rows together. Sew one post between two sashing strips together as shown in the diagram. Make eighteen.

4. Now sew a sashing strip between block 27 and 24 as shown in the diagram.

5. Repeat step 4 using these block pairings:

Row 1: Block 26 and 23
        Block 25 and 3
        Block 10 and 11
Row 2: Block 1 and 21
        Block 22 and 9
        Block 8 and 6
        Block 2 and 20
Row 3: Block 7 and 17
        Block 19 and 5
        Block 18 and 4
        Block 12 and 16

6. You now have all the pieces to put together the final quilt. Sew together in rows to create the final project as shown in the diagram on page 112.

7. Layer the quilt with batting, backing and quilt. Trim and bind.